Beyond the Basics of Computing for the Older Generation

Other Books of Interest

* * * * *

Beyond the Basics of Computing for the Older Generation

Jim and David Gatenby

BERNARD BABANI (publishing) LTD
The Grampians
Shepherds Bush Road
London W6 7NF
England

www.babanibooks.com

Please Note

Although every care has been taken with the production of this book to ensure that any projects, designs, modifications and/or programs, etc., contained herewith, operate in a correct and safe manner and also that any components specified are normally available in Great Britain, the Publishers and Author do not accept responsibility in any way for the failure (including fault in design) of any project, design, modification or program to work correctly or to cause damage to any equipment that it may be connected to or used in conjunction with, or in respect of any other damage or injury that may be so caused, nor do the Publishers accept responsibility in any way for the failure to obtain specified components.

Notice is also given that if equipment that is still under warranty is modified in any way or used or connected with home-built equipment then that warranty may be void.

© 2008 BERNARD BABANI (publishing) LTD

First Published - March 2008

British Library Cataloguing in Publication Data:

A catalogue record for this book is available from the British Library

ISBN 978 0 85934 616 0

Cover Design by Gregor Arthur

Printed and bound in Great Britain by
J. H. Haynes & Co. Ltd., Sparkford

About this Book

This book is a follow-up to our best selling title Computing for the Older Generation. Many people have by now acquired the basic computing skills and are ready to move on; this book is intended to provide the necessary help and guidance, set within the context of useful applications.

The first chapter gives an overview of the essential features of the two most popular operating systems, Windows Vista and XP. Many of the innovations in the Office 2007 software suite are then described, including the radically different *ribbon* which replaces the traditional menu bar.

Popular programs within The Office Home and Student 2007 edition are demonstrated using applications such as OneNote to organize your life and PowerPoint to illustrate a talk. The mail merge facility can save an enormous amount of time when sending out lots of standard letters and printing address labels. A straightforward mail merge which uses both Excel and Word is described. Calculations and charts in Excel are then explained using the Body Mass Index – a subject all too familiar for some of us.

Later chapters show how your computer can easily be upgraded to enable you to watch and record digital television. A separate chapter describes using eBay to get rid of surplus household items or even start a new career in online buying and selling. Another chapter shows how to keep your computer running well and finally some simple, inexpensive but useful hardware additions are discussed.

I have used Microsoft Word in the preparation of numerous books like this one and have drawn on this experience to include a chapter on the creation of longer Word documents. I hope this will help you to produce more polished newsletters, magazines, reports, etc., or better still, get your first book published.

About the Author

Jim Gatenby trained as a Chartered Mechanical Engineer and initially worked at Rolls-Royce Ltd using early computers in the analysis of aircraft engine performance. He obtained a Master of Philosophy degree in Mathematical Education by research and taught mathematics and computing to students of all ages for many years, including the well-established CLAIT computer literacy course. Since retiring from teaching he has written nearly 30 books involving computing and Microsoft Windows. These include several of the popular Older Generation series from Bernard Babani (publishing) Ltd, and in particular the best-selling book Computing for the Older Generation. David Gatenby has worked in accountancy and contributed the chapters on eBay and PowerPoint.

Trademarks

Microsoft, Windows, Windows Vista, Windows Aero, Windows XP, Windows Paint, Windows Media Player, Windows Media Center, Windows Mail, Office 2007, OneNote 2007, PowerPoint 2007, Excel 2007, Publisher 2007 and Internet Explorer are either trademarks or registered trademarks of Microsoft Corporation. Adobe Reader is a trademark or registered trademark of Adobe Systems Inc. Norton AntiVirus and Norton Internet Security are trademarks of Symantec Corporation. WinTV is a trademark or registered trademark of Hauppauge Computer Works, Ltd. eBay is a trademark or registered trademark of Google Inc. F-Secure Internet Security is a trademark or registered trademark of F-Secure Corporation.

All other brand and product names used in this book are recognized as trademarks or registered trademarks, of their respective companies.

Contents

5

Getting into Print with Word 2007   73

6

Mailshots and Labels the Easy Way   103

7

Middle-Aged Spreadsheets   123

8

Music While You Work   135

9

Watch and Record Digital Television on Your Computer

10

Buying and Selling on eBay

11

Getting the Best from Your Computer   199

12

Useful Hardware Additions   213

Index   225

Microsoft Windows Essential Features

Introduction

Previous books in the Older Generation series from Bernard Babani (publishing) Ltd explain how to get started with a new computer. For example, the best-selling book Computing for the Older Generation gives advice on buying a new machine, setting it up in your home, connecting to the Internet and starting to use it.

This new book aims to take the user on to the next stage in making the most of their computer. The contents of this book are based on useful, practical applications intended to be both helpful and relevant to older people in particular.

Everything in this book is entirely compatible with two of the most widely-used operating systems, Microsoft Windows XP and Windows Vista. In general the material should also be helpful to users of earlier Windows versions.

Microsoft Windows contains a very large number of software tools and utilities for looking after your computer. Windows also includes many useful applications programs for various tasks such as browsing the Internet, sending e-mails, drawing and painting and home entertainment. This chapter briefly outlines some of the most relevant Windows components; more detailed explanations are given in the context of the practical applications later in the book.

Windows is the operating system used on the vast majority of computers in the world. At the time of writing most new computers are supplied with either Windows XP or Windows Vista already installed. The operating system controls virtually everything such as managing the screen display of windows, menus, etc., saving and printing documents and setting up new software and hardware.

There have been many versions of Microsoft Windows over the years. Windows 3.1 was one of the earliest popular versions, then Windows 95, Windows 98, Windows Millennium, Windows XP and now Windows Vista. In the past it has generally been possible to upgrade a computer by simply installing the latest version of the Windows software, without modifying the hardware components. However, Windows Vista introduces some major changes compared with Windows XP and represents a major leap forward. This is mainly because of the greatly enhanced 3D graphics facilities in Vista.

This means that some older computers are not powerful enough to run Windows Vista; in some cases it may be possible to modify an older machine by fitting new components to bring it up to the Vista standard.

Users of both Windows XP and Windows Vista should be able to follow the work in this book with confidence; all of the material is relevant to both Windows XP and Windows Vista computers.

Applications Software in Microsoft Windows

Applications software in this context refers to stand-alone programs which can be used for tasks such as drawing and painting or managing accounts, etc. In contrast, *systems software* and *utilities* (discussed shortly) are used in the running of the computer and for "housekeeping" and maintenance tasks.

Windows contains the following applications software of particular relevance to this book, namely:

- Internet Explorer
- Windows Mail
- Windows Paint
- Windows Media Player
- Windows Media Center

The above Windows components are probably already installed on your computer and can be accessed from the Vista **Start** and **All Programs** menu as shown below.

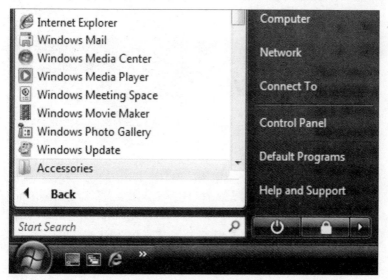

Internet Explorer

This is a Web browser – a program used to find and display Web pages. The latest version, Internet Explorer 7, was introduced as standard on Windows Vista and can also be used with Windows XP (a free download is available).

Internet Explorer 7 introduces many improvements over earlier versions and has been well received by the computer press. One of the new features is *tabbed browsing* which allows several Web pages to be open at the same time; switching between Web sites simply involves clicking on tabs at the top of the screen.

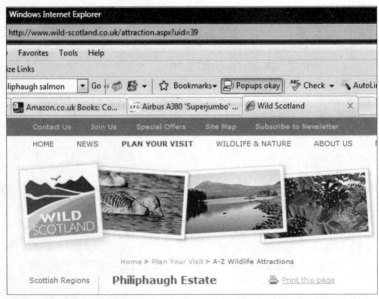

The example above shows tabs for three Web sites currently open in Internet Explorer. The tabs are **Amazon.co.uk...**, **Airbus A380 'Superjumbo'...** and **Wild Scotland**. Switching between sites happens instantly as soon as a tab is clicked.

E-mail

Both Windows XP and Windows Vista have their own e-mail programs, called Outlook Express and Windows Mail respectively. The general methods for using both programs are the same. The E-mail program is launched from the **Start** menu or the **All Programs** shown on menu on page 3.

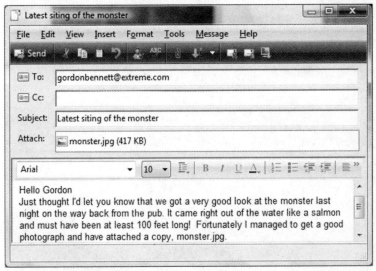

Apart from being able to send messages including text and pictures, you can also send *attachments* to e-mails, such as copies of photographs; a relative online in Australia, say, could download and print the photographs almost immediately. You can also send documents as e-mail attachments. Office Word 2007 allows you to save documents as *PDF (Portable Document Format)* files. These can be read by many different types of computer and certainly those equipped with the widely used Adobe Reader software (downloadable free from the Internet).

Windows Paint

Although there are many more sophisticated graphics programs available, **Paint** in Microsoft Windows is a useful tool for drawing, painting and editing images. It is launched from the **Accessories** menu, as shown on page 3, after clicking **Start** and **All Programs**.

As can be seen above, **Paint** has a limited set of drawing tools; these can be used to create your own artwork for insertion in documents in Microsoft Word or Publisher, for example. **Paint** can also be used to resize photographs or *crop* them by removing surplus areas around the outside. Images can be saved in, or converted to, a variety of file formats such as the JPEG photographic format, often used for images sent to the Internet.

The Windows Media Player

The Windows Media Player is launched from **Start** and the **All Programs** menu as shown on page 3. Currently on version 11, the Windows Media Player turns your computer into a versatile music and video centre. You can copy a whole library of music, currently on CDs, onto your hard disc. Favourite tracks can be organized and saved in *playlists*. Then you can listen to your music whenever you want, without having to find and insert the CDs.

Music can be played with the Media Player in the background while you are working away at some other task on the computer such as creating a document. Music downloaded to your computer from the Internet can be "burned" onto a CD or portable MP3 player and listened to while you are on the move or away from the computer.

As shown along the bottom of the Windows Media Player illustrated above, there is a full set of controls operated by the mouse, including **Play**, **Pause**, **Stop**, **Next**, **Previous**, **Mute**, **Volume**, **Turn shuffle on** and **Turn repeat on**.

The Windows Media Center

The Windows Media Center takes the home computer a step nearer to being at the heart of a complete home entertainment system, including music, DVDs and watching and recording television. The Windows Media Center software is included with Windows Vista Home Premium and Vista Ultimate; the Windows XP Media Center Edition has been available for a few years. The program is launched from **Start**, **All Programs** and **Windows Media Center**, as shown on page 3.

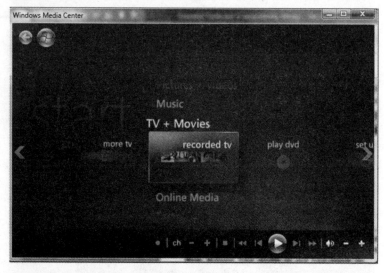

In order to record television programs your computer needs to be fitted with a device called a *TV tuner*. You will also need space on your hard disc to store programs. It's possible to buy ready-made *Media Center PCs* containing all of the necessary components for a complete home entertainment centre. As discussed later, however, a modern PC can be modified easily and cheaply to serve as a capable Media Center PC.

Windows Utility Software

This section outlines some of the software needed to change settings on your computer and carry out routine "housekeeping" tasks to keep it running efficiently.

The Control Panel

The **Control Panel**, accessed from the **Start** menu, is used for installing and deleting software, for setting up new hardware devices like mice and printers and for changing settings such as the screen display.

The **Control Panel** can also be used to ensure that the **Windows Firewall** is switched on, to prevent anyone from gaining access to your computer for malicious purposes. Familiarity with the **Control Panel** is essential if you want to change the settings on your computer and manage the installation and removal of software and hardware.

The Device Manager

This is launched from the **Control Panel** shown on the previous page. In Vista click **Start, Control Panel** and double-click the icon shown on the right. XP users should double-click the **System** icon in the **Control Panel** and then the **Hardware** tab and the **Device**

Device Manager

Manager button. The **Device Manager** opens, displaying a list of all of the hardware devices on your computer.

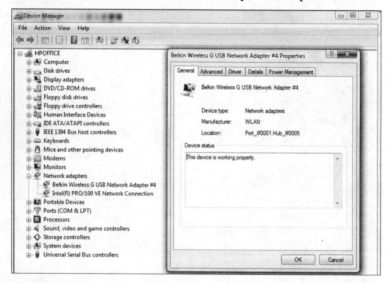

Double-clicking a heading such as **Network adapters** above expands the list to show the two adapters fitted to this particular computer. Double-clicking a device launches the **Properties** window shown on the right above. This states whether the device is working correctly and allows you to update the *device driver*. A driver is a piece of software which enables a hardware device such as a printer to work with a particular version of Windows, such as XP or Vista.

System Tools

This feature contains some of the tools needed to keep your computer running efficiently. It is launched by clicking **Start, All Programs, Accessories** and **System Tools.**

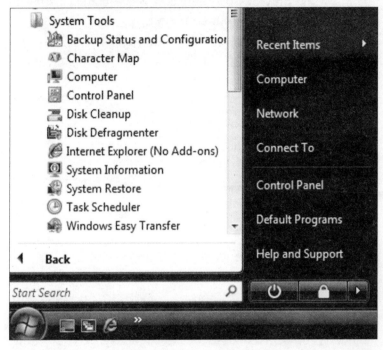

Disk Cleanup and **Disk Defragmenter** are two of the main tools for maintaining your hard disc and are discussed in detail later in this book. A number of the items listed in the above menu, such as the **Control Panel** and **Internet Explorer** can also be launched from the **Start** and **All Programs** menus, as previously discussed.

Computer listed above is a Windows Vista feature which displays all of the disc resources on the computer. (**My Computer** is the corresponding Windows XP feature).

Easy Transfer is a method of copying files between computers across a network, via a special USB Easy Transfer cable or by using CDs, DVDs or USB flash drives. **System Information** shown on the **System Tools** menu on the previous page gives a very detailed listing of all of the resources in your computer.

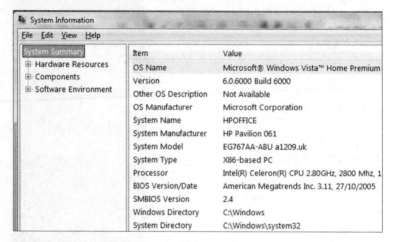

System Restore

When your computer is working well it's possible to take a "snapshot" of the critical settings. This can be initiated manually or scheduled to occur regularly. The resulting collection of settings is known as a *restore point* and is saved for future use. Restore points can be scheduled automatically or manually by clicking the **Create** button in **System Protection** within **System Restore**. If something goes wrong with your machine, perhaps after installing new software or hardware, you can revert to the restore point to apply previous settings which are known to be good. It's therefore recommended that you create a restore point before making major alterations to your computer.

Windows Update

This feature, launched from **Start** and **All Programs**, enables you to download from the Internet the latest modifications to the Windows software and install them on your computer. Such modifications, often called "patches", might, for example, be intended to close a breach in the security of the Windows operating system. This could potentially allow "hackers" to gain access to your computer and possibly steal financial or personal information.

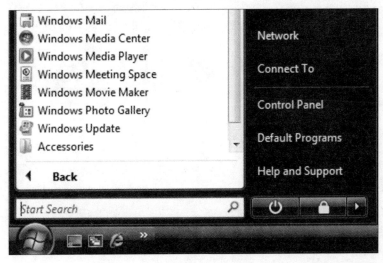

You can schedule your computer to check for updates at a certain time every day. Updates are downloaded from a Microsoft Web site; you are told which updates are available and can choose whether to download and install individual updates to your machine. When version 11 of the Windows Media Player was launched, it was available for downloading as an automatic update for users of Windows XP. (The Windows Media Player version 11 is provided as standard in Windows Vista).

Relaxing with Windows Games

If working at your computer has left you stressed out, you can always unwind with some of the games built into Windows XP and Vista.

The Windows games can be launched after clicking **Start**, **All Programs** and **Games**. Vista users can also simply click **Games** on the right of the **Start** menu.

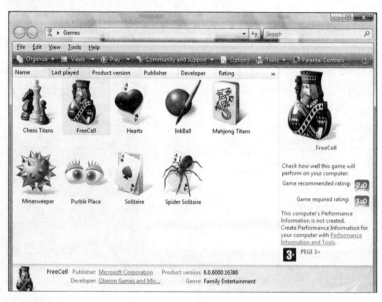

A variety of games are provided in Windows such as the arcade-type Minesweeper, various versions of the Solitaire card game and Chess Titans in which you play against the computer. Some of the games include instructions and a choice of levels of difficulty.

Research has shown that continued participation in mentally-challenging activities (such as computer games) lowers the risk of degenerative brain disease in older people.

Introducing Office 2007

Introduction

Microsoft Office has dominated business computing for many years. It's known as an *integrated software suite* and includes the essential office software, i.e. word processing, database (record keeping) and spreadsheet (number crunching, accounts, graphs and charts, etc.)

The latest version, Office 2007, comes in several flavours to suit different the types of user, from large organizations down to people working at home on their own. The Office Professional version, for example, includes more programs than the Home and Student edition, as shown below.

	Microsoft Office Basic 2007	Microsoft Office Home & Student 2007[1]	Microsoft Office Standard 2007	Microsoft Office Small Business 2007	Microsoft Office Professional 2007	Microsoft Office Ultimate 2007 NEW!
Microsoft Office Word 2007	●	●	●	●	●	●
Microsoft Office Excel 2007	●	●	●	●	●	●
Microsoft Office PowerPoint 2007		●	●	●	●	●
Microsoft Office Outlook 2007	●		●			
Microsoft Office Outlook 2007 with Business Contact Manager [2]				●	●	●
Microsoft Office Publisher 2007				●	●	●
Microsoft Office Access 2007					●	●

Office Home and Student 2007 can be obtained for as little as £80, while the Professional and Ultimate editions can cost over £500. Prices vary between suppliers so it's worth doing some comparison shopping on the Internet. It's also worth checking to see if there's an *upgrade* edition of the software available. This will be considerably cheaper but requires an earlier "qualifying" version of the software to be already installed on your computer.

Office Home and Student 2007

Many home users will find that the Office Home and Student 2007 meets all their needs. As shown on the previous table, full versions of the world-beating Word and Excel programs are included. The Access database is not included but many home users will find that the Excel spreadsheet can double up as a competent filing system. Also provided are the PowerPoint 2007 presentation software and OneNote 2007, a program for organizing information from different sources and in various formats. A single copy of Office Home and Student 2007 may be installed on up to 3 machines, recognizing the fact that many homes now have more than one computer.

Any edition of Office 2007 is classed as qualifying software for an upgrade version of Publisher 2007, which can be obtained for about £80. The Office Home and Student software, together with the software included in Windows XP and Vista, such as Internet Explorer 7, Paint and the Windows Media Player and Media Center, can help to create a very useful and versatile computer. This software, in Windows Vista and XP and also Office 2007 Home and Student Edition, should meet the needs of the majority of computer users and is the basis of most of the applications in the rest of this book.

Installing Office Home and Student 2007

The Office Home and Student 2007 package consists of a plastic box containing the software on a single CD. A label containing bar codes should appear on the top of the box to indicate that the copy of the software is genuine. There is also a list of minimum hardware and software requirements needed to run the software, namely:

- 500MHz or faster processor
- 256MB RAM
- 1.5MB available hard disc space
- CD-ROM or DVD drive
- 1028x768 or higher resolution monitor
- Windows Vista or XP with Service Pack 2

The packaging also contains a note stating that the software is licensed for use on 3 computers.

The Product Key

On the back of an inner plastic case in the package is the PRODUCT KEY label. This is your licence to install the software – without it you can't validate and activate the software. It's worth making a copy of the 25-character key and storing it in a safe place. You might have a technical problem later and need to re-install the Office software – a task which is impossible without the product key.

At the bottom of the CD itself is a hologram in which the word **GENUINE** alternates with the word **MICROSOFT**. In an age when counterfeit software production is rife, it's important to use only genuine software. Users of illegal copies of software often find they can't install the latest software upgrades or get telephone support.

During the installation process you will be asked to enter your 25-character product key – letters must be in upper case. If you don't enter a product key you will only be able to use the software for a limited time, e.g. 30 days.

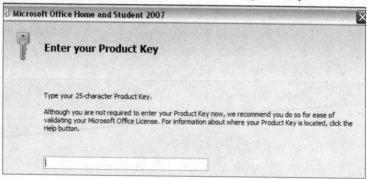

If the product key is genuine, a green tick appears and you then click **Continue** to carry on with the installation. After choosing to either **Upgrade** or **Customize** you are presented with a window showing the **Progress** of the installation as a percentage. Finally you are informed that the software has been successfully installed and you can, if you wish, **Go to Office Online** to get updates, help and online services.

As with many software installations, you need to restart the computer before using the software for the first time.

Activation

Microsoft Office has to be *activated*, a process intended to prevent single-user editions of software being installed on more than one computer. (Office Home & Student 2007 is an exception, being licensed for up to 3 installations). During the installation process you are given the choice to activate over the Internet or by telephone. If you don't activate your copy of Office you will only be able to use the software for a limited time.

Launching the Programs

At the end of the installation process you will find entries for **Microsoft Office**, including **Word** and **Excel**, in the **All Programs** menu accessed via the **Start** orb in the bottom left-hand corner of the screen as shown below.

Any of the component programs of Office Home & Student 2007 can now be launched by clicking their entry in the **All Programs** menu shown above. As shown on the next page, a new, radically different "user interface" has been introduced in Microsoft Office 2007 and this has been applied to the Word, Excel and PowerPoint programs.

The Tabbed Ribbon

Gone are the traditional drop-down menus such as **File**, **Edit** and **View**, etc., to be replaced by a *tabbed ribbon* as shown below. Ribbons are used in Word, Excel and PowerPoint.

All of the usual tools are still available – it's just that they are presented in a different layout. On the ribbon there are various tabs such as **Home**, **Insert** and **Page Layout**, as shown above. Icons and tools for particular tasks are grouped together, such as the **Font** group for changing the style and size of letters. The text formatting tools such as indentation, centring, justification and line spacing are displayed in the **Paragraph** group shown above.

One of the most striking features of the ribbon is that as you change to a different task, the tools on the ribbon change automatically. For example, if you select a picture or image so that it's highlighted in a Word document, the **Format** tab with **Picture Tools** above it, appears as shown below. Clicking this tab displays a complete set of tools for formatting a picture. An extract from the ribbon displaying the **Picture Tools** on the **Format** tab is shown below.

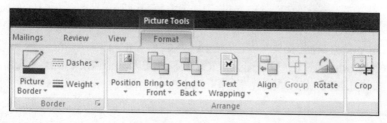

If you now deselect a picture by clicking within the main text of a Word document, the ribbon reverts to the text editing tools on the **Home** tab, shown in the extract below.

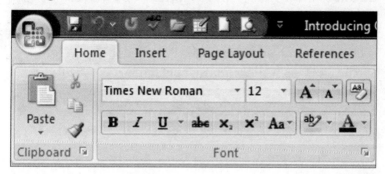

Please note the small arrow in the bottom right-hand corner of the **Font** group shown above. Clicking this arrow launches the **Font** dialogue box, giving a comprehensive range of settings as an alternative to the ribbon **Font** group.

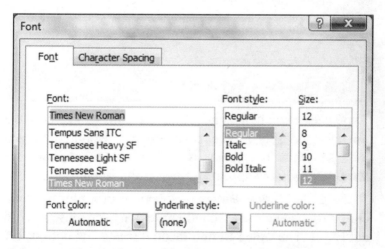

Other groups such as **Paragraph** and **Styles** have similar dialogue boxes accessed by an arrow on the bottom right corner of the group.

The Office Button

If you allow the cursor to hover over the **Office Button** (shown right) in the top left-hand corner of the screen, a small help window appears, as shown below. The **Office Button** is used for major tasks such as saving and printing a Word document or Excel spreadsheet, as well as for opening a new document.

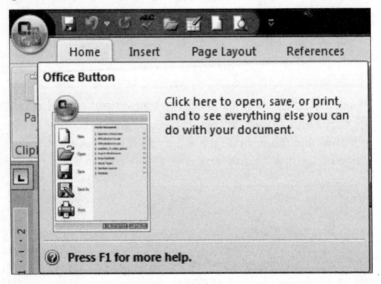

If you need extra help at any time, press the **F1** key near the top left-hand side of the keyboard. For example, if you press **F1** while the cursor is over the **Office Button**, the **Word Help** window appears giving further support.

Clicking the **Office Button** displays a drop-down menu similar to the **File** menu found in previous versions of Word and Excel. The **Office Button** menu displays the options for major tasks, such as saving and printing your work and starting a new document, as shown on the next page.

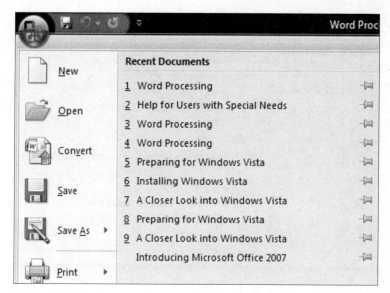

Saving Documents in Various File Formats

The **Save As** option shown in Word 2007 can be used to save documents in a number of different file formats, as shown on the next page. These include:

Word Document (.docx)

The **.docx** format was introduced in Word 2007. To read **.docx** files into earlier versions of Word, download the Office Compatibility Pack from Microsoft Office Online.

Word 97-2003 Document

Save in this format if you want to create documents which can be opened in earlier versions of Word. Word 2007 can open documents created in earlier versions of Word.

PDF (Portable Document Format)

This is a universal format which can be read on any type of computer, using a program called Adobe Reader, available as a free download from **www.adobe.co.uk**.

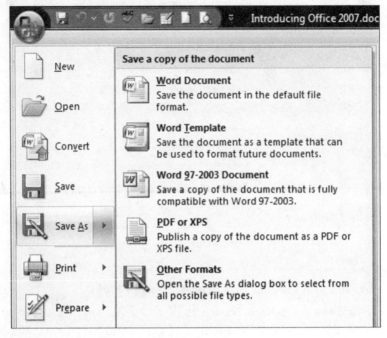

Displaying File Name Extensions

Shown on the right are two files displayed in the Windows Explorer. **doc** is the file name extension for documents saved in earlier versions of Word. **docx** is the file name extension for Word 2007 documents. To display the file name extensions in Explorer

Using ebay.doc   Using ebay.docx

open a window by double-clicking the **C:** drive in the **Computer** or **My Computer** feature in Windows. Select **Tools** and **Folder Options...** or (in Vista only) **Organize** and **Folder and Search Options**. Click the **View** tab and make sure **Hide extensions for known file types** is not ticked. The file name extensions should now be displayed in Explorer.

Zooming In and Out of an Office Document

It's often useful to be able to zoom in to get an enlarged view of part of a document in Word or Excel. Or in a longer document you may want to zoom out to see several pages side by side on the screen, as shown below.

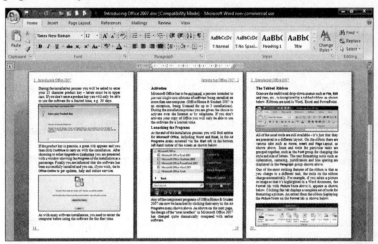

The **Zoom** slider on the status bar at the bottom right-hand corner of the screen in Office 2007 is a very convenient tool for zooming in and out of documents in Word, Excel and PowerPoint. Drag the slider or click the **+** or **–** buttons.

Additional zoom controls appear on the **View** tab on the ribbon, with options to display one or two pages, full page width, or specify a %, including a button for 100%.

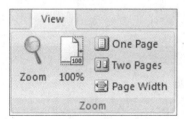

The Quick Access Toolbar

At the top left of the screen, to the right of the **Office Button**, is the **Quick Access Toolbar**.

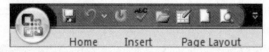

The **Quick Access Toolbar** is a set of icons representing frequently used tasks such as saving a document, undoing the last operation, checking spelling or starting a new document. These icons provide a very fast way of performing common tasks; for example, regularly clicking the disc icon shown on the right is a convenient way to quickly save a document without changing the file name, file type or folder on your hard disc, etc. (To change these details you need to use the **Save As** option from the **Office Button**.)

Tool icons can be added or removed from the **Quick Access Toolbar** after clicking the small arrow to the right of the toolbar, shown below.

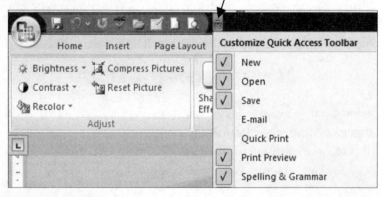

Now click the tool, to add or remove the tick in the **Customize Quick Access Toolbar** panel shown above right.

Programs in Office Home and Student 2007

Previous pages discussed the new interface with which users interact with Office 2007. This included the new tabbed ruler and its groups of tools which change to suit the work being done. There is also the new **Office Button** and corresponding menu for doing important tasks such as saving and printing; the zoom slider is a very quick way to change the size of the view on a document. These innovations provide a common interface for three of the main Office 2007 programs, namely Word 2007, Excel 2007 and PowerPoint 2007.

The following pages give an overview of the programs found in Office Home and Student 2007; these can be launched from the **All Programs** menu off the **Start** button, as shown below.

After you've used a program you will find it listed in the **Start** menu, so that you no longer need to open the **All Programs** menu.

The programs listed above play a major part in the applications later in this book.

Introducing Word 2007

Word processing is one of the most frequently used applications of computers and Microsoft Word is the undisputed world leader. The modern word processor is capable of creating all sorts of documents, such as:

- Letters to friends and relatives
- Reports including tables and graphs
- A newsletter for a club or parish magazine
- College reports such as a thesis or dissertation
- A novel or book (such as this one) as shown below.

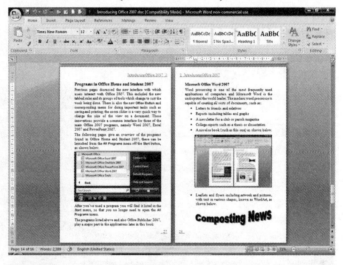

- Leaflets and flyers including artwork and pictures, with text in various shapes, known as WordArt, as shown below.

Advantages of Word Processors

Word processors are far more versatile than the traditional typewriter; they are easy to use and allow anyone to produce professional-looking documents. Some of the advantages of the word processor are as follows:

- Corrections can be made on the screen before printing on paper, so there is no evidence of any alterations. Several copies can easily be printed.

- Documents are saved on disc and can be retrieved later. This allows a document to be used again, perhaps with small changes such as a new date. There is no need to retype the whole document.

- Text can be *edited* more easily – whole blocks of text can be inserted, deleted or moved to a new position in the document.

- The *Find and Replace* feature enables a word (or group of words) to be exchanged for another word (or words), wherever they occur in a document.

- Text can be formatted with effects such as bold and italic and in various fonts or styles of lettering, such as the Algerian font shown below.

ALGERIAN

- The layout of the page can easily be changed or with text set in tables or newspaper-style columns.

- Modern word processors contain many additional features such as spelling and grammar checkers, a thesaurus and a word count facility.

Introducing Excel 2007

Excel is the leading spreadsheet program; it is designed to work on tables of figures, reducing long and complex calculations to simple point and click operations using a mouse. Excel 2007 is operated using a new ribbon interface, very similar to the one used in Word 2007.

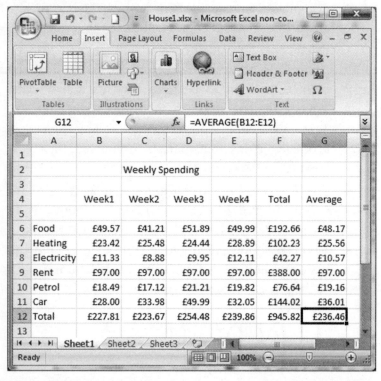

As shown in the applications later in this book, Excel can also be used as a filing system for storing records such as names and addresses.

Recalculation

The spreadsheet allows you to speculate on the effect of possible changes, such as an increase in the price of petrol. These changes can be fed into the spreadsheet, which automatically recalculates all of the totals, etc., affected by the change. The *recalculation* feature is one of the main advantages of spreadsheet programs and can save many hours of work compared with traditional methods of calculation using pencil and paper or pocket calculator.

Graphs and Charts

Apart from the ability to perform the whole range of mathematical calculations, data can be presented in the form of pie charts, bar charts and line graphs, etc.

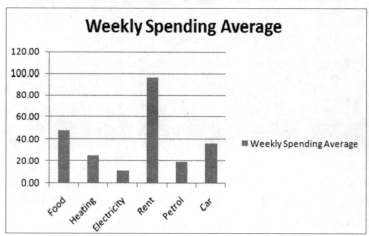

Both the spreadsheet itself and the charts produced from it can be imported into documents in a word processor. This feature is useful, for example, when producing a report on sales performance in a business.

Excel 2007 is discussed in more detail in extended applications later in this book.

Introducing PowerPoint 2007

PowerPoint is widely used for presentations to large audiences but is also a very convenient tool for creating interesting family slide shows or to illustrate an informal talk to a club or group of friends. PowerPoint 2007, like Word and Excel, uses the new Office 2007 ribbon layout for the various tools, as shown below.

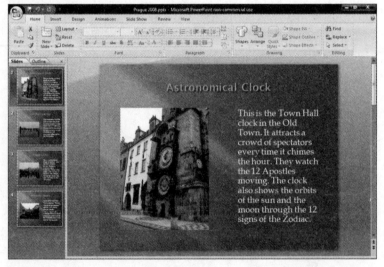

PowerPoint is used for creating "slides" consisting of separate pages of text, graphics and multi-media. The slide show would normally be viewed on one or two monitors or projected onto a screen. You can add sound such as a commentary and the slides can be moved on automatically or under the control of a mouse. Many different templates and graphical designs and animations are available to give the presentation a very stylish and consistent appearance.

A PowerPoint presentation can be viewed on the Internet or sent across the world as a file attached to an e-mail.

Introducing OneNote 2007

OneNote is a program for organizing information from many sources and in many different formats. Then it is immediately accessible in one place – a virtual "notebook" stored on your computer. There is no longer any need to search for bits of paper, Web addresses, Web pages, Word files, video clips, etc., scattered about your home, office or in different locations on your computer.

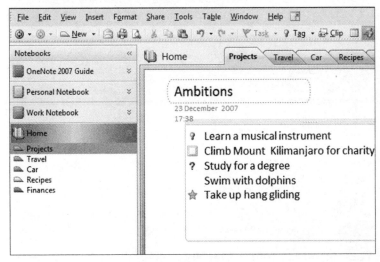

OneNote has its own built-in search facility and can even recognize and search the text within a scanned picture.

The program is very popular with students, researchers, project managers and anyone who needs to gather information. OneNote can also be used to good effect in the home, to organize holidays, hobbies, or perhaps a small business. For example, it's a simple matter to create to-do lists then flag the most important tasks and filter them out.

OneNote first appeared in 2003 and is now part of Office Home and Student 2007. It can also be bought separately for use with Windows Vista or XP.

The OneNote screen displays several "notebooks" down the left-hand side. Across the top are tabs for different sections of each notebook. Each section can have numerous named pages, listed down the right-hand side. You can create, delete and rename notebooks, sections and pages.

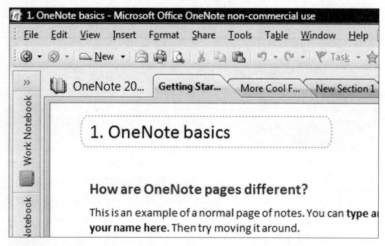

You can insert into a OneNote page all sorts of pictures, extracts from Web pages, sound and video clips, files from programs like Word and Excel, etc., and hyperlinks to Web pages. It's also easy to create your own original content on a page; this can be text which you type in or sketches made with OneNote's built-in drawing tools. Calculations can be performed on the page as you type and you can record your own audio notes. OneNote pages and sections can be e-mailed and shared with other people.

You don't have to worry about saving notebooks, sections and pages – OneNote does this automatically.

Introducing Publisher 2007

Microsoft Publisher is a program for creating professional-looking documents such as leaflets, flyers, business cards and greeting cards, etc. Publisher 2007 is included as a component program in the more expensive versions of Office 2007, such as Office Professional 2007 and Office Ultimate 2007. If you buy Office Home and Student 2007, Publisher 2007 is not included. However, Publisher 2007 is available as a separate program and an *upgrade* version can currently be bought for under £80. You can install the upgrade version if your computer already contains an earlier edition of Publisher or a *qualifying edition* of Microsoft Office such as Office Home and Student 2007.

Installation of Publisher 2007 requires the entry of a 25-digit product code, found on the inside of the plastic case in which the Publisher CD is supplied. Installing the software simply involves placing the CD in the CD/DVD drive and following the instructions on the screen. The process is very similar to the installation of Office 2007, described on pages 17 and 18 of this book. In order to make full and unlimited use of all of Publisher's features, the program has to be *activated* by telephone or by the Internet. Activation by the Internet can be achieved in just a few seconds.

While Microsoft Word is an extremely powerful and versatile program, especially for producing longer documents, Publisher 2007 concentrates on the design of shorter documents, as shown in the extract on the next page. Publisher 2007 provides hundreds of ready-made *templates* for virtually every conceivable purpose such as advertisements, calendars, business cards, e-mails, Web pages and greeting cards. The templates can be customized by inserting your own words in place of the text provided.

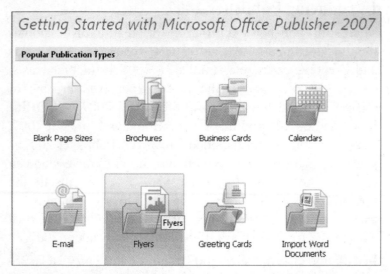

If you don't want to use the template approach, you can start off with a blank page and use the many text editing and graphical tools provided in Publisher 2007 to create your own publication from scratch.

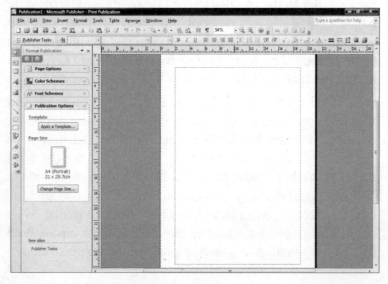

Getting Organised With OneNote 2007

Introduction

Many of us keep handwritten lists and Post-it notes scattered all over our home or office; bits of paper in drawers, business cards in wallets, and useful Web sites in the Favorites feature on our computer.

OneNote 2007 is a program designed to gather all of this information together in one immediately accessible place. OneNote was introduced in 2003 and is now supplied as part of the Home & Student, Ultimate and Enterprise editions of Microsoft Office 2007. You can also buy OneNote 2007 as a separate program for £60–£80 for use with Windows Vista and Windows XP. A trial version of OneNote can be downloaded free from the Web site:

http://office.microsoft.com

As shown by the list on the next page, OneNote is far more than a replacement for the handwritten personal organizer in a ring binder; OneNote can store notes and information in virtually every possible format – text, pictures, Web pages, hyperlinks, e-mails and audio and video clips.

OneNote is very popular with researchers, business people and anyone who handles information from many different sources; it can also help to "declutter" your mind by organizing your daily life more efficiently.

OneNote 2007 includes the following features:

- A series of electronic *notebooks* divided into *sections*; each section can have many *pages*.

- You create, rename and delete your own notebooks, sections and pages. Pages can be any size.

- Notes can be typed anywhere on the page and freely moved around in their own box or *container*.

- The page can contain text, pictures, tables, voice recordings and video clips, handwriting, e-mails and links to Web pages. Personal sections can be *password protected*.

- Files such as Word documents can be inserted as *attachments* in a OneNote page. The file is opened in its associated program by double-clicking.

- The pages are *searchable* for *keywords*; this includes words embedded in scanned images such as business cards containing text.

- A *clipping* feature allows you to "grab" areas of a Web page and place them on a OneNote page.

- Calculations can be performed easily in OneNote while you are typing the text on a page.

- Colleagues can collaborate using *shared notebooks*.

- Pages from OneNote can be e-mailed to friends or posted on the Internet.

- Tasks in your notes can be marked with *tags* such as **Important** or **To Do**. Tasks with a particular tag can be quickly identified when needed.

- All of the notes and information are saved automatically – there's no need to remember to carry out a separate saving operation.

Using OneNote 2007

To launch OneNote for the first time, select **Start**, **All Programs**, **Microsoft Office** and **Microsoft Office OneNote 2007**.

Subsequently you can launch OneNote directly from the **Start** menu. OneNote opens with some sample notebooks already set up. As can be seen below, three notebooks are listed down the left-hand side of the screen. Tabs across the top represent different sections of the currently selected notebook. Down the right-hand side is a list of the pages in the current section.

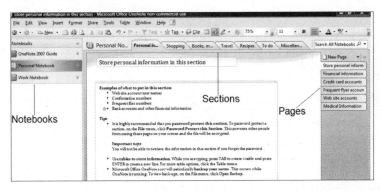

Referring to the screenshot on the previous page, you can see three notebooks listed down the left-hand panel. These are the **OneNote 2007 Guide**, a **Personal Notebook** and a

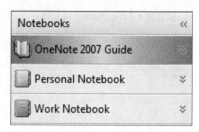

Work Notebook as shown on the right. Clicking the chevron-like arrows to the right of the word **Notebooks** above displays all the notebook names vertically, instead of horizontally, up the left-hand side of the screen.

If you click the chevrons to the right of one of the notebook names, a list of sections within that notebook appears. For example, clicking **Personal Notebook** expands the notebook to display **Personal information**, **Shopping**, **Books**, etc. If you click the chevrons again, the list of sections collapses.

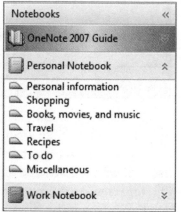

Notebooks, sections and pages can easily be created, renamed and deleted, as discussed shortly.

The sections in the current notebook are displayed in tabs across the top of the screen, as shown below.

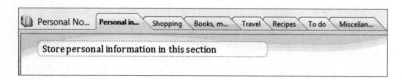

To have a look at what's in a particular tab, click the tab name, such as the **To do** tab shown below and at the bottom of the previous page.

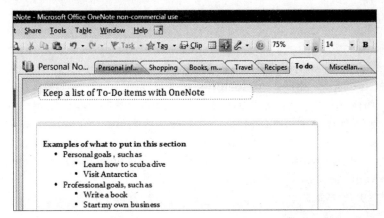

You can create as many new pages as you like in a section and give them suitable names. Shown on the right are the pages for the **Personal information** section of the **Personal Notebook** shown earlier.

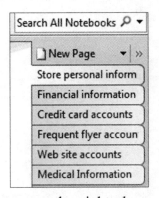

New Page shown on the right allows you to insert extra blank pages into the current section. There is also a choice of templates with ready-made layouts and headings to suit certain situations such as meetings and lectures.

The **Search All Notebooks** bar shown on the right above allows you to enter keywords. Using optical character recognition, OneNote will find the keywords if they occur in any notebook, even if they are part of a scanned image such as a picture or business card imported into OneNote.

The OneNote 2007 Guide

Before starting to create your own notebooks, sections and pages, it's a good idea to have a look at the OneNote 2007 Guide. The guide has itself been produced in the form of a OneNote notebook and is one of the sample notebooks displayed when you first start using OneNote. The first section, **Getting Started with OneNote**, has 12 pages explaining different features of the program. If you read through all of the pages in the guide and experiment by selecting different pages, tabs and notebooks, you should soon get an overview of the software. Then you can start creating your own notebook(s), as discussed in the remainder of this chapter.

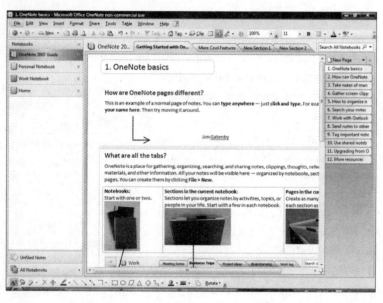

Creating a New Notebook

The next few pages show how to set up a new notebook in OneNote. The notebook, called **Home**, will have three sections, called **Projects**, **Travel** and **Car**. In practice the notebook would be much bigger, with more sections and more pages per section. However, this simple example should suffice to demonstrate most of the skills needed.

Click the arrow to the right of **New** and select **Notebook...** from the drop-down menu which appears, as shown on the right. Then you are asked to give a **Name** to the new notebook and also select a template 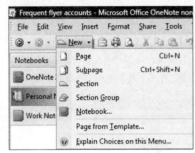 such as **Personal Notebook** shown below. There is also a chance to choose a background colour.

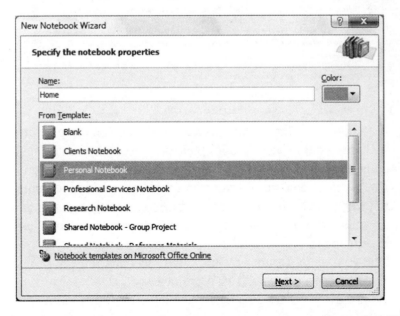

If you choose a template, such as **Research Notebook**, for example, the new notebook (called **Science** in this example), will have several ready-made sections such as **Data collection** and **Brainstorm**, shown on the right. In the **Data Collection** section there is a page called 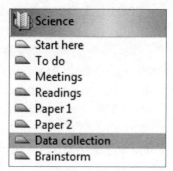 **About this section**, giving examples of what you might put in the section. You would delete these notes and replace them with your own material.

Examples of what to put in this section
* Research questions
* Investigation methods
* Study limitations
* Field notes
* Key observations.

Tips
* You can **record an interview** and take notes at the same time. The audio/video recordings are automatically embedded as a file in your notes. To begin an audio recording, on the Insert menu, click Audio Recording.
* The search feature (CTRL+F) will search for words in audio recordings as well as text and images.
* Try using a table to organize your data in OneNote 2007. You can copy and paste your tables into Microsoft Office Excel spreadsheets.
* Keep your research data and notes in one place by **inserting files** directly into this section. You can insert any file type into your notes and edit those files directly from your notes. To insert a file, on the Insert menu, click Files.

As shown in the notes above, the OneNote page can include your own notes, plus audio/video recordings embedded as files on the page. There is a search feature which can scan all of your notebooks and find certain keywords, even if the words are buried in audio recordings or scanned images. Files from other programs such as Word and Excel can also be inserted as icons into the OneNote page. Double-click the icon to open the file in its associated program such as Word or Excel.

For the simple **Home** notebook, we can start by choosing **Blank** from the **New Notebook Wizard**, shown earlier. After clicking **Next** the wizard asks, **Who will use this notebook?** and you respond by selecting **I will use it on this computer**.

When you move on by clicking **Next** again, the wizard displays the default location where the new notebook will be automatically saved, in this case:

C:\Users\Jim\Documents\OneNote Notebooks

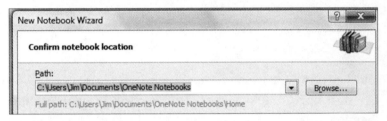

Alternatively, click **Browse...** to save the new notebook in a folder of your choice. Knowing the save location is helpful if you are used to managing your files in the Windows Explorer, My Computer or Computer features in Windows XP or Windows Vista, as shown below.

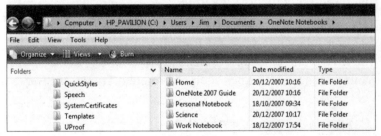

Here you can manage the notebooks and sections like any other folders and files. This is done by right-clicking over a folder and selecting operations like **Cut**, **Copy**, **Rename** and **Delete** from the drop-down menu which appears.

After confirming the location for saving the notebook, click **Create** and OneNote displays a blank page in a new section.

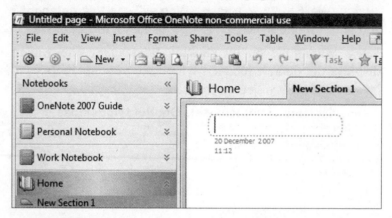

At this stage, the notebook **Home** consists only of **New Section 1**, which OneNote has created automatically. From the original brief, we had sections **Projects**, **Travel** and **Car**.

Click the arrow next to **New** and select **Section** from the drop-down menu. Another tab **New Section 2** appears next to **New Section 1** shown above. Repeat this until you have the required number of sections.

It's now just a case of right-clicking each of the **New Section** tabs and selecting **Rename...** from the drop-down menu which appears. Replace **New Section 1**, etc., with your own section names such as **Projects**, **Travel** and **Car**.

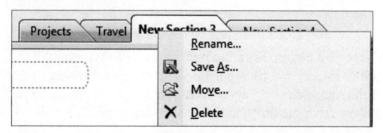

Creating New Pages

When you start a new section in OneNote there is a blank page ready for you to begin typing text and adding various types of information, such as pictures and links to Web sites. Initially the blank page will appear in the list of pages in the right-hand column as **Untitled page**. However, an empty slot is provided at the top left-hand corner of the page; here you enter the title for the new page such as **Garden Projects**. On pressing the **Enter** key, this page title also appears in the right-hand column as shown below.

To add further new pages click the arrow next to **New Page** shown on the right and select **New Page**. Another blank page appears with a blank slot ready for you to enter a page title, as shown below.

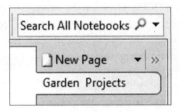

In this example, **Building Work** was entered as the title for the second page. This appeared in the right-hand column of OneNote, as shown on the right. The **Projects** section in the **Home** notebook now has two new blank pages, **Garden Projects** and **Building Work**.

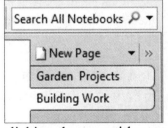

You can move between pages by clicking the page titles, as shown above. Any number of pages can be created in a section and you can make the pages as big as you like.

Entering Text

To return to the **Garden Projects** page, click the title in the right-hand column and start entering text. The OneNote page allows you to enter text freely anywhere you like; it is automatically surrounded by a *container* or frame, which expands to suit your

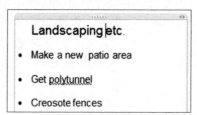

text. When you've finished entering text the entire container can be dragged around the page, after clicking in the bar at the top of the container. This is very useful for annotating notes with labels and moving them into position.

OneNote has a set of text formatting tools across the top of the screen, such as the font style and size, bold, underline and bullets, as shown in the toolbar extract below.

To start a second block of text on a page click anywhere you like and start typing. A new container appears, expanding as required to suit the text.

Writing and Drawing Tools

OneNote has a large selection of pens and highlighters which can be used with the mouse for freehand writing, drawing and also highlighting text. From the **Tools** menu, select **Writing Tools**, **Pens** and choose from the list of **Felt Tip Pens** and **Highlighters**.

Select **View**, **Toolbars** and **Drawing Tools** to display a set of tools for drawing straight lines, circles, rectangles, etc., as shown below.

Inserting a Picture

To insert a picture, click roughly where you want the top left-hand corner of the picture to be. This is not too critical since you can easily move and resize the picture later.

Now select **Insert** form the Menu Bar at the top of the screen and then **Pictures** from the drop-down menu.

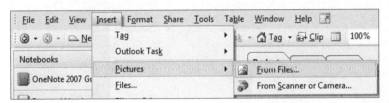

You can now choose to insert a picture **From Files....** This picture might be in a folder on your hard disc, on a CD/DVD or perhaps on a USB data dongle. The **Insert Picture** window opens allowing you to locate the required picture. Click the **Insert** button to place the picture on the OneNote page. As shown above, the source of a picture can also be a scanner or digital camera.

Initially the picture may be too big or in the wrong position. Move the mouse cursor over the edge of the picture so that a cross made from four arrowheads appears. Click the mouse and a set of eight "handles" appears around the perimeter of the picture.

The picture can be resized by dragging any of the corner handles. The position of the picture can be adjusted by dragging the picture with the left-hand mouse button held down. The picture of the dahlia is shown in place below.

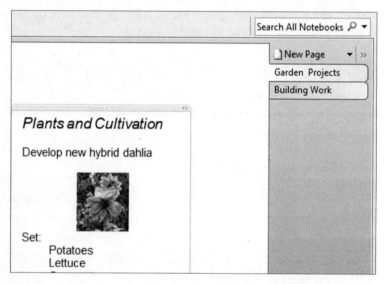

It's now just a case of selecting the title **Building Work** in the right-hand column to open that new blank page and begin entering the text and any other information.

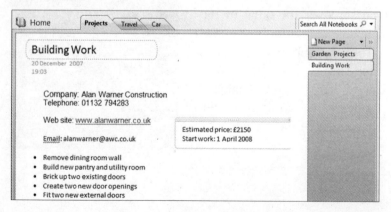

Inserting a Live Web Link into a OneNote Page

Please note in the previous screenshot that you can type a Web address onto the OneNote page. This address becomes a live link to the Web site (of the builder, in this example), so you don't need to switch to the Favorites feature.

E-mailing a OneNote page

If, for example, you want to e-mail the builder to query a point in the notes, you could quickly type in your question and e-mail the whole lot. Simply click the envelope icon on the toolbar at the top of the screen, as shown below.

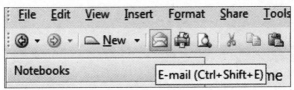

Your e-mail program opens with the OneNote page (**Building Work** in this example) attached in two formats; as a Web page and as a OneNote page.

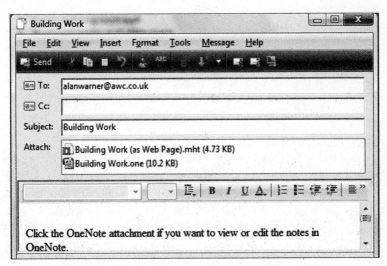

On reading the e-mail, the Web page version of the
OneNote page will be displayed in full; the page in the
OneNote format is included as an attachment and can be
read in OneNote. A link is included for the person
receiving the e-mail to obtain a free trial copy of OneNote.

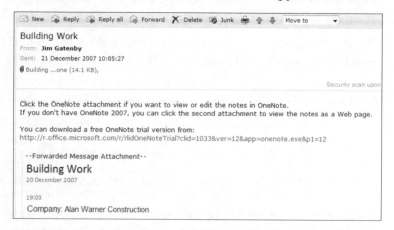

OneNote pages can be exported to other programs by
selecting **File** and **Send To**, as shown below.

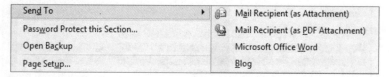

As shown above, OneNote pages can also be sent to an e-
mail recipient as a PDF (portable document format)
attachment. This is a widely-used format for saving
documents so that they can be read on any brand of
computer, using the Adobe Reader software, freely
downloadable from **www.adobe.co.uk**. OneNote pages can
also be sent to Microsoft Office Word for inclusion in a
document. The final option is to send the OneNote page to
a Blog (or online diary) for viewing on the Internet.

Using Tags to Mark Notes

When you create a list of notes you might want to mark some as important, for example. Place the cursor next to the note you want to tag. Then click the arrow next to the word **Tag** on the toolbar across the OneNote screen. From the

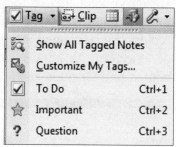

menu which drops down, click the tag you want to use. A small sample of the available tags is shown above.

In the extract from the **Garden Projects** page shown on the right, **Get polytunnel** has been tagged as **Important** and **Repair greenhouse** is marked **To Do**. Click a **To Do** check box to place a tick in the box to indicate completion of a task.

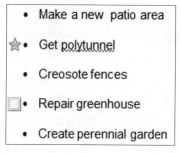

Tags can be removed by placing the cursor next to the note and clicking the tag entry in the **Tag** menu shown at the top of this page.

Viewing Tagged Notes

From the **Tag** menu shown at the top of this page, select **Show All Tagged Notes**. The **Tags Summary** panel appears on the right-hand side of the screen, listing each of the tags used and the notes to which the tags have been applied.

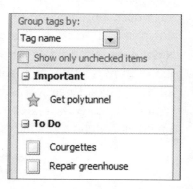

Copying Scanned Images into OneNote

If you've kept lots of recipes in scrapbooks, it's a simple job to scan them and save them in OneNote. The following recipes were scanned into the Paint program, which is part of Microsoft Windows. After editing in Paint they were copied into OneNote using **Edit/Copy** and **Edit/Paste**.

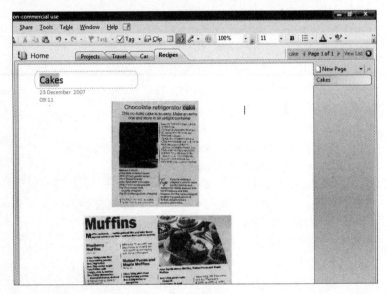

Searching in OneNote

You can search for keywords anywhere in OneNote. A drop-down menu next to **Search All Notebooks** allows you to search the current section, notebook or all notebooks. Even words buried

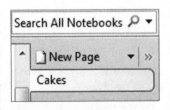

within an image in a scanned document, e.g. **cake,** will be found and highlighted in colour in the OneNote page.

Chocolate refrigerator **cake**
This no-bake cake is so easy. Make an extra
one and store in an airtight container

Inserting a Screen Clipping into OneNote

You can "grab" any area of the screen and paste it into OneNote. For example, with a Web page on the screen, hold down the Windows key (shown left) and press the **S** key. A small cross appears which can be dragged to enclose the required screen area in a rectangle. When you release the left-hand mouse button, the **Unfiled Notes** tab opens automatically with the Web screen clipping already on the page.

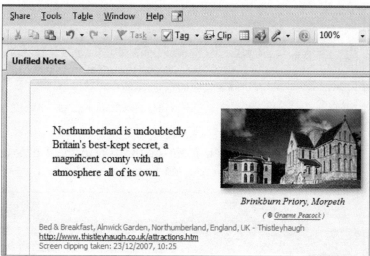

A live link to the Web site appears on the OneNote page.

You can display your screen clippings by clicking the **Unfiled Notes** button at the bottom left-hand side of the screen. Each screen clipping occupies a separate page.

To place the screen clipping on another OneNote page, select the clipping and use **Edit/Cut** or **Copy** and **Edit/Paste**.

Accessing Files from OneNote

You can insert links to files in OneNote; for example, suppose you need to keep looking up information in an Excel spreadsheet or a Word document. Select **Insert** and **Files...** from the OneNote menu bar. Then browse for the files in the folders on your hard disc, as shown below.

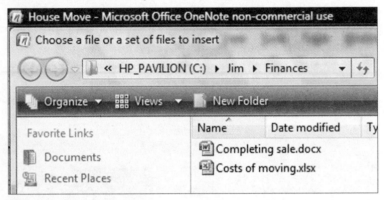

Click **Insert** to embed an icon for the file in the OneNote page, as shown by the Word and Excel examples below.

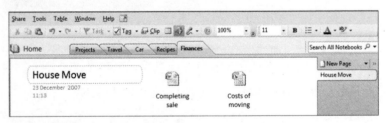

Calculations in OneNote

You can perform a calculation at any time in OneNote while you're in the middle of typing. For example, if you type **39*47=** and then press the space bar, the answer **1,833** appears immediately.

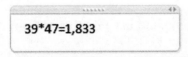

Password Protection in OneNote

Personal and financial information can be protected in OneNote by applying a password to a section. Passwords cannot be applied to embedded audio and video files and you cannot search within a protected section.

To apply a password to the currently selected section, click **File** and **Password Protect this Section:**. After clicking **Set Password...** you are required to enter and confirm your password. Passwords in OneNote are case-sensitive.

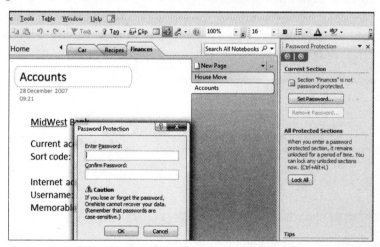

Passwords should be impossible to guess, at least 8 characters long and preferably contain a mixture of numbers and letters. You are warned that if you lose your password you will not be able to recover the data in the protected section. If you enter a section protected by a password, the right-hand panel displays options to change or remove the password, as shown on the right.

Including a Voice Recording in OneNote

You can add a spoken commentary to a OneNote page; for example, to quickly add some extra notes or explanations. All you need is a cheap microphone connected to the sound input socket on your computer.

Select **Insert** from the Menu Bar across the top of the OneNote screen, then click **Audio Recording** from the drop-down menu which appears.

A new container appears on the page with the title of the current page (**Ambitions** in this example) below an icon which include the letters **WMA** (Windows Media Audio file). A note below states when the sound recording started.

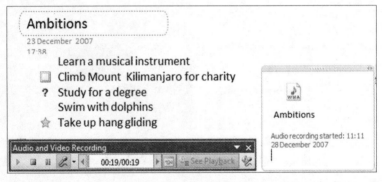

As shown above, the OneNote page also displays a small on-screen audio and video recorder, with controls for starting and stopping a recording. When you've finished a voice recording, click the stop button. The recording can be played back by double-clicking the **WMA** icon and clicking the **Play** button on the on-screen player which appears.

The OneNote **Insert** menu also has an option to insert a video recording, if you have a suitable camera connected to your computer.

Putting on a Show with PowerPoint

Introduction

PowerPoint is supplied as part of most versions of Office 2007, including Office Home & Student 2007. PowerPoint is a program used to illustrate the key points of a talk or lecture, by producing "slides" which can be viewed on a computer monitor. The slides are really just separate screens, which can be moved on at the click of a mouse; alternatively you can set up a slide show with the slides changing automatically after a specified time. A slide can contain text, pictures and photographs as well as flowcharts and multi-media sound and video clips. Animations can be added to liven up a presentation.

In the case of a lecture to a large audience, the slides may be projected onto a screen or second monitor. **Presenter View** in PowerPoint allows additional notes and prompts to be added which only appear on the presenter's monitor, not on the second screen viewed by the audience. Slides can also be printed on paper and used as handouts.

Although PowerPoint has typically been used for lectures and business meetings, it can equally be used for an informal talk to a smaller group such as friends and family or a club or society. Or you could e-mail a PowerPoint presentation to a friend for viewing on their computer.

Getting Started with PowerPoint

PowerPoint is launched by selecting **Start**, **All Programs**, **Microsoft Office** and **Microsoft Office PowerPoint 2007**, as shown below. The next time you want to use PowerPoint it will be listed directly on the main **Start** menu.

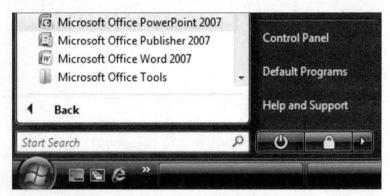

PowerPoint opens and you can immediately see that it has a new style ribbon similar to the one in Word 2007, instead of the traditional Menu Bar used on many earlier programs.

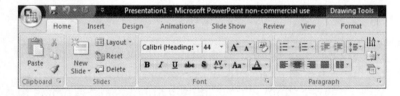

As can be seen above, the PowerPoint ribbon has a number of tabs such as **Home**, **Insert**, **Design**, **Animations** and **Slide Show**. Each tab is divided into several groups of icons, such as the **Slides** and **Font** groups shown above. The icons within each group represent various tools and operations, such as formatting, editing and design.

Creating a Slide Show

Working in Normal View

Normal View is the first screen you see when you launch PowerPoint from the **Start** menu.

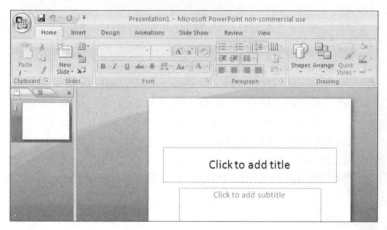

In the main section is the template of the slide, where you can start to add a title, pictures and text. This slide is also shown as a thumbnail image under the **Slides** tab in the left-hand panel. As further slides are created, their thumbnails are displayed in the left-hand panel.

The **Outline** tab shown on the right displays the text for all of the slides in the presentation.

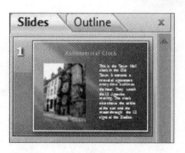

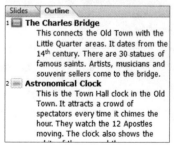

Changing the Template

The default template is a very simple layout and this can easily be changed; for example, you might want to include a photograph, some text and a title. To select a new template, click **New Slide** in the **Slides** group on the PowerPoint ribbon as shown on the left. This reveals a choice of templates for your slide, as shown below. It really depends on what you want to include in your design; some templates only allow a title, whereas others enable text, photos and a title as well as multi-media clips such as sound and video. In this chapter, a slideshow is created to illustrate a trip to Prague, based on the **Two Content** template shown in the extract below.

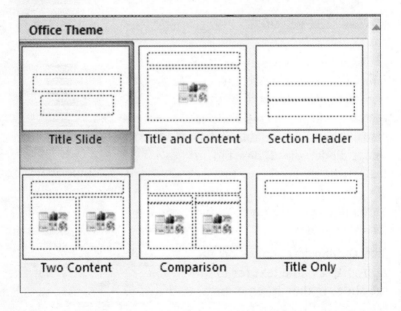

Inserting a Title

Simply type in an appropriate title for the slide; the text can be changed using the **Font** group on the ribbon. There are also icons which enable you to add a shadow effect or to change the colour of the letters.

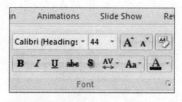

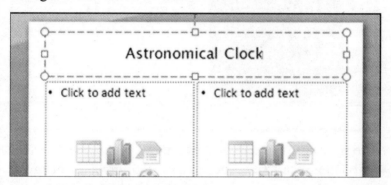

Inserting a Picture from a File

To place a picture into the slide, click on a position on the template where you want the picture to be. Then go to the **Insert** tab on the PowerPoint ribbon and click the **Picture**

icon, as shown on the left. The **Insert Picture** window opens, allowing you to browse your computer for the required picture. Select the picture and click the **Insert** button and the picture is placed on the slide in the selected frame, as shown on the next page.

Click inside the picture to select it, so that eight handles appear; it can now be moved or resized by dragging.

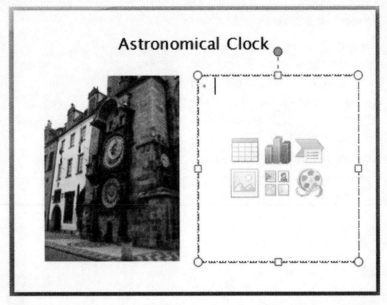

The six icons on the right above allow you to insert various objects into the frame, such as a chart or graph, a picture or a sound or video clip, for example. The bottom left icon is **Insert Picture from File**, so we could have clicked on this to insert our photo of the Astronomical clock. It doesn't matter which method you use – quite often there are a number of different ways of doing the same thing.

So now we have a title and a picture for this particular slide. To complete the slide, we need to add the notes about the Astronomical clock; simply type the information into the frame, after selecting a suitable font and letter size.

The notes on the slides are the key points which will be seen by the audience; the speaker can also use **Presenter View** to add additional notes to act as prompts; these will not be seen by the audience.

Astronomical Clock

This is the Town Hall clock in the Old Town. It attracts a crowd of spectators every time it chimes the hour. They watch the 12 Apostles moving. The clock also shows the orbits of the sun and the moon through the 12 signs of the Zodiac.

We now have a completed slide, with text added. The next step is to add another slide. To do this, go to the **Slides** group on the ribbon and click on **New Slide**. A new template will appear. Continue to produce the rest of your slides as previously described. As you continue to create new slides they appear as thumbnails on the **Slides** tab on the left-hand side of the **PowerPoint** screen.

Editing a Slide

To edit a particular slide, click the thumbnail of the slide in the **Slides** tab shown on the right. The text can also be edited in the **Outline** tab, which shows the text for all of the slides.

Viewing a Slide Show

To start a slideshow, select the **Slide Show** tab from the ribbon at the top of the PowerPoint screen. If you click **From Beginning**, your slide will fill the screen and the slideshow will start, although it may be necessary to press a key or click the mouse to move between slides. A more effective way to view the slideshow is to use the **Rehearse Timings** facility. This enables you to set the show to run automatically using predetermined times for each slide.

This is particularly useful if you wish to talk more about certain topics than others. You work out how long you will discuss each slide during the presentation and PowerPoint records the time taken; these timings are saved and used for the actual presentation.

To set the timings for a presentation, select **Rehearse Timings** as shown on the right. Your first slide will appear and in the top left-hand corner, a timer starts recording the duration of the slide. You would then begin   your presentation. Once finished, click the arrow and the next slide appears. If you are not happy with these timings, you can reset the clock by clicking on the **Undo** arrow on the timer and begin again. At the end of this rehearsal, a total time taken will be displayed. PowerPoint allows you to accept this as the time duration to be used in your actual presentation. The timings are then set up for your presentation. It's then just a case of selecting **From Beginning** from the **Slide Show** tab on the PowerPoint ribbon and the slideshow will run at your chosen speed.

Sorting Slides into Order

Once you've created a series of slides, you may wish to change the order of them. Go to the **View** tab on the ribbon and select **Slide Sorter** in the **Presentation Views** group, as can be seen to the left below.

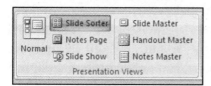

Your set of slides appears as shown below. You then drag the slide(s) to the required position.

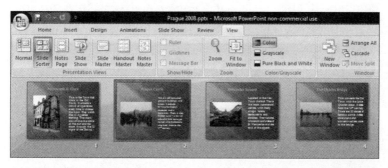

Slides can be moved by dragging from left to right; to move a slide from right to left, drag the slide on its left from left to right. The slideshow on the sights of Prague can be seen above. I originally wanted to discuss the Astronomical clock first, but now wish to start with The Charles Bridge, so the slides were re-arranged by dragging. The new sequence is shown below.

Headers and Footers

As in a Word document, headers and footers, such as the time and date can be placed on slides. Select the **Insert** tab on the ribbon and then click the **Header & Footer** icon. A menu appears as shown below, with a list of options and check boxes allowing you to choose what to include on the slides. The date is set by default and will be updated automatically so that whenever you do the presentation, the current date is always displayed. You can also include slide numbers if you wish. Tick **Footer** and type in a suitable footer to appear at the bottom of the slide.

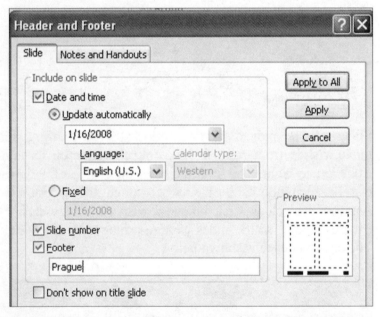

Once you are happy with the settings, click **Apply to All**.

Inserting Animations

To make your presentation more interesting, it's possible to include special effects or animations in between slides. Simply go to the **Animations** tab and you will see a group of patterns; these are the animations which allow each new slide to make a dramatic entrance onto the screen.

If you scroll down using the arrows shown above on the right, there are lots more animations to choose from. To test the animation, simply click on it. **Apply To All** shown below adds the animation to every slide in the presentation.

To accompany the animations, you can add sound effects after clicking the arrow to the right of **Transition Sound** on the **Animations** tab shown below. There is a large variety of different sounds from chimes to a noisy explosion and they can certainly liven up a presentation. You can also adjust the speed of the changeover using the **Transition Speed** setting **Slow**, **Medium** or **Fast**.

The **Advance Slide** option gives a choice between clicking the mouse to advance the slides or setting them to change automatically after a specified time, for example five

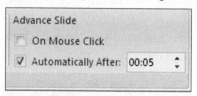

seconds, as shown on the ribbon extract on the left. Click **Apply To All** on the **Animations** tab to ensure that the animation effects are applied to all slides.

To have a look at the finished slide show, including all of the animations and sound effects, click the **Slideshow** tab on the ribbon and then click **From Beginning**.

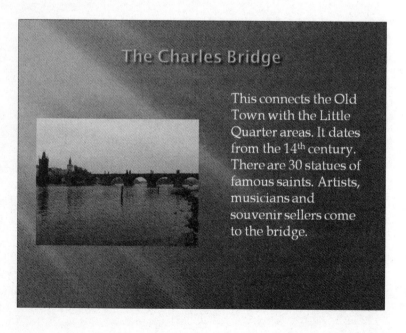

Presenter View

To use this facility you need to have two monitors set up for the presentation. One monitor, viewed by the audience, just displays the basic PowerPoint presentation. The person giving the presentation has their own monitor, not visible to the audience; this displays not only the basic presentation but also any notes, prompts and information to help the presenter. **Presenter View** is accessed by going to the **Slide Show** tab on the PowerPoint ribbon and selecting **Use Presenter**

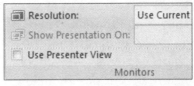

View in the **Monitors** group. When you select **Presenter View**, you are given the chance to check if your computer can be used with multiple monitors. Desktop computers normally need a second graphics card to be installed in order to utilise two monitors; many laptop computers have the technology needed to run two monitors already built in.

Changing the Colour Scheme

Slides are created on a white background by default, but this can be changed easily. Select the **Design** tab and the **Themes** group presents a choice of several different colour schemes for the slide. Click on each of the designs shown in miniature below and the main slide changes accordingly.

Inserting SmartArt Graphics

A PowerPoint slide can include charts and graphics. A simple example would be a flowchart outlining the steps to take when planning a holiday. This can be done very easily by inserting a few key words into readymade graphics provided in the **SmartArt** facility shown below.

The **SmartArt** icon appears in the **Illustrations** group on the **Insert** tab on the ribbon as shown on the right. There is a vast array of different flow chart designs to choose from. In the design below, known as the **Basic Cycle**,

each circle initially contains the word **Text**. Simply type your own words into the circles, replacing the word **Text** in each circle. The **SmartArt** graphic can occupy a whole slide based on the blank template or it can be placed within a frame in a slide containing text and other information.

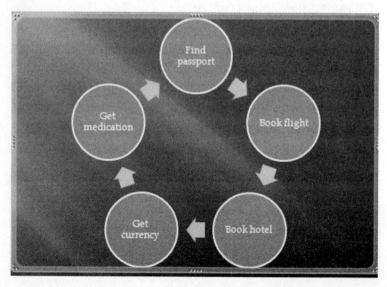

5

Getting into Print with Word 2007

Introduction

Most of us only scratch the surface when using the world's leading word processor, Microsoft Office Word 2007, as it's currently known. Word 2007 is at the heart of all of the versions of Microsoft Office 2007.

Word in various editions has been the most popular word processor in offices for many years, churning out memos, letters, reports, etc. However, Word is capable of much more creative work, ranging from a short leaflet containing fancy lettering and graphics to a full size book consisting of hundreds of pages. Despite its power and versatility, Word remains very easy and enjoyable to use – it's the software by which other brands of Word processor are judged.

I've used Word for the creation of over 20 books, such as this one, from composing the first draft to producing the final typescript on a CD, ready to send to the printers.

This chapter is intended to help the reader use many of the features in Word which I have found particularly useful.

The material in this chapter should be useful for the creation of longer documents such as:

- A newsletter consisting of several pages
- A parish or club magazine
- A history of your town or village
- A dissertation for a degree you are taking
- A report presenting your case in a dispute over environmental, safety or planning issues
- A textbook based on the knowledge and experience acquired during your working life
- The novel you always wanted to write.

These longer documents require a few more skills over and above those needed to produce the more usual short memo or letter. Topics covered in this chapter include:

- Creating a page design template on which to base documents in order to give a consistent layout
- Setting the default font, paper size, margins, paragraph formatting and line spacing in a template
- Inserting headers, footers and page numbers into a template
- Using text boxes in a document
- Inserting pictures, photos and other images into a document
- Moving, resizing and cropping various types of image in a document
- Capturing all or part of the computer screen, including Web pages, for insertion into a document.

The Page Design

Publishing companies use professional page designers to produce a specification to suit the intended readership. For example, these Older Generation books are set in a large type for easy reading. The page design also sets the font styles and sizes for headings, sub-headings, body text, and contents and index pages. A frequently-used style employs Times New Roman for the main body text, with Arial for sub-headings.

When producing a document which you hope to get published, it's a good idea to look at some high quality examples in the same field as yours. It may be difficult to improve on the designs of professionals who've had years of experience. The page layout for an Older Generation book is shown below. This illustrates some of the main features to be discussed shortly.

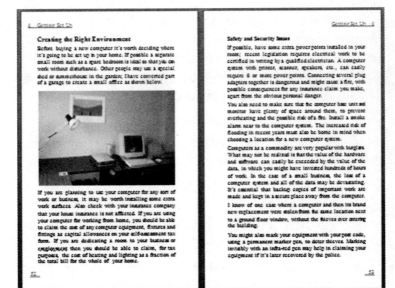

In the page layout on the previous page, *mirror margins* have been used. Instead of left-hand and right-hand they are referred to as *inside* and *outside* margins. The wide inside margins are often necessary in a book or magazine to compensate for the binding. Please also note that the chapter headings at the top of the page are mirrored, on the outside of both even and odd numbered pages. Similarly the page numbers appear on the outside of both even and odd pages.

Creating a Template

The page layout settings can be saved as a Word *template*; every time you start a new document you open a blank page based on the template, with all of the settings for margins, headers and footers, etc., already built in. Although you can apply all of the formatting, etc., to a *document* as you enter the text, using a template ensures a consistent page layout; for example, each time you produce a newsletter or magazine. In the case of a book, each new chapter might be started from the template and saved as a separate document file. If you don't select a template when you open a new document, the **Normal** template is used by default. A new template is created as follows:

1. Open a blank page in Word.

2. Apply all the settings for fonts, line spacing, margins, paper size, headers and footers, page numbers, etc., for your chosen page design.

3. Save the page as a Word *template* not a *document*.

4. To start a new document requiring this layout, select the new template and open a blank page.

5. Enter the text and any pictures and in future continue saving this piece of work as a *document*.

Setting the Default Font

Open a new blank page by clicking the **Office Button** and then **Blank document** and click **Create** at the bottom right. The blank page opens in Word, based on the default template **Normal.dotm**. The task now is to apply the settings for the new page design to this blank page, then save it as a template, not a document.

By default, Word 2007 starts up with the **Calibri** font style in size **11pt**. Most of my work is done using **Times New Roman** size **12**. To change the default font, with the **Home** tab selected, click the small arrow in the corner at the bottom right of the **Font** group, shown below.

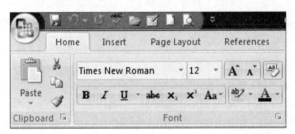

The **Font** dialogue box opens, allowing you to select the font style and size.

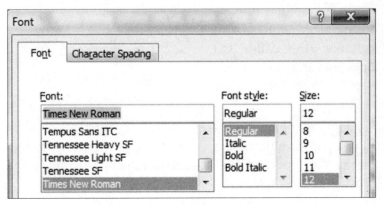

To make the selected font into your default font, select the **Default...** button at the bottom left of the **Font** dialogue box. The following window appears, warning that this new default font will apply to all future documents based on the **NORMAL** template. This includes any templates which we create from a blank page.

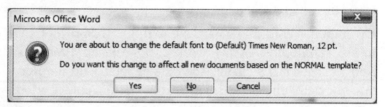

If you click the **Yes** button shown above, all new documents will open with the new default font, **Times New Roman** in this example.

Text in Columns

If you are creating a newsletter or magazine, which uses a 2 or 3 column layout throughout, it will help to set this up in the template. From the **Page Layout** tab select **Columns** and

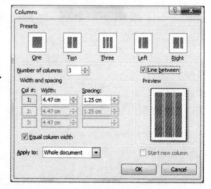

More Columns.... As shown on the right, the **Columns** dialogue box opens, allowing you to select the **Number** of columns, the **Width** and **Spacing** and to include vertical lines between the columns.

To apply a column layout to just part of a document, it would be necessary to do this during the typing of the document rather than during the creation of a template.

Setting the Page Margins

From the Word 2007 ribbon select the **Page Layout** tab, then click the small arrow shown below in the bottom right-hand corner of the **Page Setup** group.

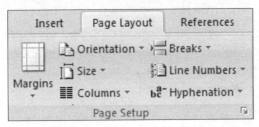

This opens up the **Page Setup** dialogue box shown below. If you want a wide inside margin and a narrow outside one, (similar to this book), select **Mirror margins** from the drop-down menu next to **Multiple pages** shown below. For the Older Generation books, the inside margins are set at **1.7cm** with outside margins of **1.2cm**.

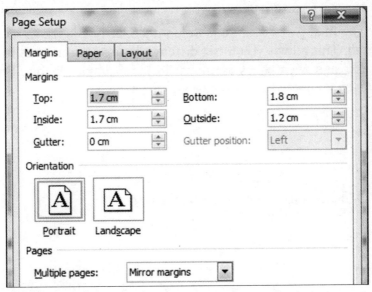

Setting the Paper Size

The paper size is specified after selecting the **Paper** tab shown on the **Page Setup** dialogue box below and on the previous page. If you are using standard paper such as A4, select the size from the drop-down menu next to **Paper size**.

The Older Generation books are printed on paper which is 13cm wide and 19.8cm high, so **Custom size** is selected as shown below and the exact measurements in centimetres entered for **Width** and **Height**.

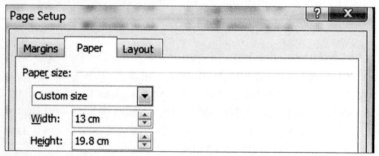

Headers and Footers

The final part of the **Page Setup** dialogue box is the **Layout** tab. This allows you to set different headers and footers for odd and even pages as shown in the examples below. On even numbered pages the header is on the left:

> 4   Getting Set Up
>
> If you go to one of the big stores they will sometimes "bundle" a complete package to include a printer, modem

Odd pages have the header on the right:

> Getting Set Up   4
>
> With the small local business, if you do have problems it should only be a matter of returning the machine for

To achieve this, select the **Layout** tab shown below and make sure **Different odd and even** is ticked under the words **Headers and footers**.

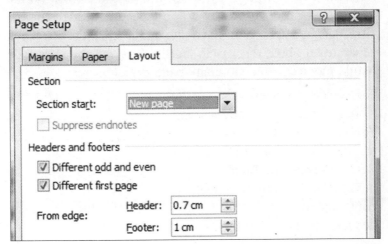

Referring to this book, you can see that the first page in every chapter has a large chapter title, but unlike the other pages in the chapter, doesn't have a small header containing the chapter heading. To achieve this, in the **Layout** tab as shown above, make sure **Different first page** is ticked. The entries **0.7cm** and **1cm** against **Header** and **Footer** above refer to the distances from the top and bottom of the paper.

Please note that the above settings in the **Page Setup** dialogue box can also be made from the **Design** tab on the Word 2007 ribbon, as shown below.

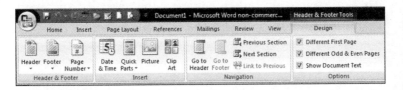

Entering the Text for the Headers

At this stage we have a blank page with a number of built-in settings for the page layout. Still basing the work on the Older Generation books, we don't need a header for the first page as this will have the main chapter title in a separate text box, discussed shortly. Leaving the first page blank, move to a second blank page, which is even.

Now select **Insert** from the ribbon and the **Header and Footer** group appears on the ribbon, as shown on the right. Select **Header** and **Blank** and the header is highlighted with a 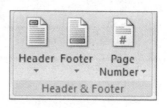 container ready for you to enter the text for the even page header, in this example, **4 Getting Set Up**.

Now move down to the next blank page which should be odd and enter the odd page header, on the right this time.

Footers are created in a similar way to headers, after selecting **Footer**, as shown above in the **Header & Footer** group on the Word 2007 ribbon. Then click **Blank**.

You may wish to add some horizontal lines or perhaps a logo to give a bit of style to your headers and footers. These features will then appear automatically on every page throughout the document.

Inserting Page Numbers

In these books, the footer is only used for the page number. If you are placing the page numbers on the outside of each page, as in this book, you will need to set up the page numbers on both the first odd and the first even page in the template. If you've selected **Different first page**, as discussed earlier, you will need to create a three page template with page numbers inserted on the first page (odd), the second page (even) and the third page (odd). Once you start typing a long document based on the three page template, Word automatically increments the page numbers 4, 5, 6, etc.

To insert a page number, select **Page Number** from the **Header & Footer** group on the Word ribbon, shown on the previous page.

You are given a choice of position on the page for the page numbers, top, bottom, in the page margins or at the current cursor position, as shown on the menu on the right below.

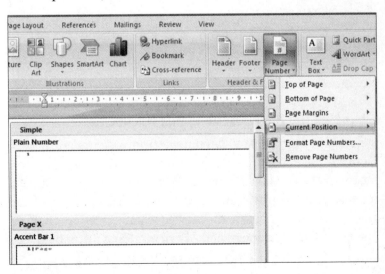

For each position for the page number, top, bottom, etc., there is a choice of styles, such as colour, italics and to include the word **Page** as a label or to enclose the number in brackets. Click on your chosen style such as **Plain Number** or **Accent Bar 1** shown on the previous page and the page number is placed on the template. Repeat this for the first two or three pages of the template, depending on whether **Different first page** has been selected in the **Layout** tab of the **Page Setup** dialogue box as discussed earlier and shown again below.

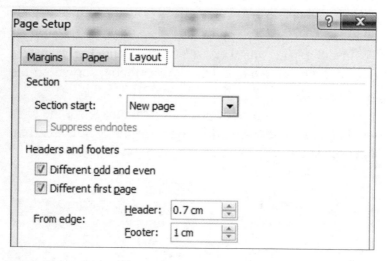

Changing the Page Numbers in a Document

When you start a new document from a template it will begin at page 1. However, in this book, for example, each chapter is created as a separate document and each chapter must start with a different page number. The number of the first page of a document can be changed after clicking **Insert**, **Page Number** and **Format Page Numbers** as discussed in detail in the section Creating a Document.

Line Spacing

When producing book or magazine, you will probably want to keep a consistent amount of space between lines of text. This can be set in the template after clicking the small arrow to the right of word **Paragraph** in the Word 2007 ribbon shown below.

This opens the **Paragraph** dialogue box, where apart from setting **Tab** stops and **Indentations**, you can set the **Line spacing**. The drop-down menu includes choices such as **Single** or **Double Spacing**. Choosing **Exactly** allows you to specify the space between lines in *points* as in **14pt** shown below. The point is an old printing measurement – there are 72 points in one inch.

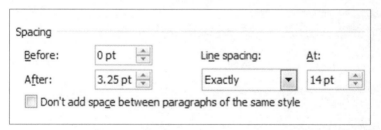

As shown above, you can add space before and after paragraphs; in the example above, **3.25pt** will be added after every paragraph. I frequently insert **6pt** in the **Before** slot, to give a bit of daylight between a picture and the next paragraph.

Saving a Template

You don't have to specify every setting on the template but it does save time and ensures a consistent design through a series of newsletters, magazines or a book such as this one.

From the **Office Button** select **Save As** then enter a suitable name for the template, such as **Hang Gliding News**. Make sure **Word Template (*.dotx)** is selected. If you are likely to need the template on machines which don't have Word 2007 installed, select **Word 97-2003 Document (*.doc)** from the drop-down menu next to **Save as type**.

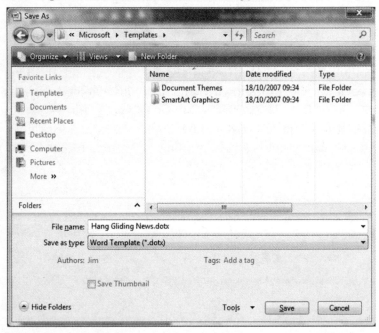

Now click **Template**s, as shown above on the left and click the **Save** button and your new page design is saved in your **Templates** folder.

Creating a Document

You will need the new template whenever you start a new document which requires that particular design; for example, producing the latest edition of a newsletter or magazine or when starting a new chapter in a book.

To start a new document based on the template, click the **Office Button** and select **New**. (Don't use the **New** icon on your **Quick Access Toolbar**, at the top left of the screen, as this will launch the default template **Normal.dotm**).

After selecting **New**, under **Templates** on the left-hand panel, click **My templates...**. Now choose the required template, such as **Hang Gliding News.dotx** shown below. Make sure **Document** is selected under **Create New** shown below on the right and, click **OK**.

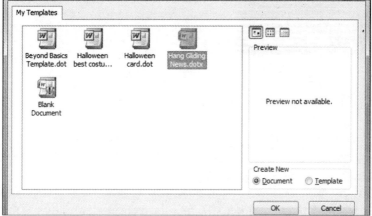

A new blank page opens containing all your page layout settings, ready for you to start work.

Changing the Page Numbers in a Document

When you open a new document based on a particular template, it will normally start at page 1. This may not always be what you want; in this book, for example, each chapter is created and saved as a separate document or file.

So each document or chapter starts with a different page number. To change the page number of the first page of the document select the **Insert** tab on the Word 2007 ribbon. Then select **Page Number** and **Format Page Numbers....** The **Page Number Format** dialogue box opens, allowing you to change the page number in the slot next to **Start at**.

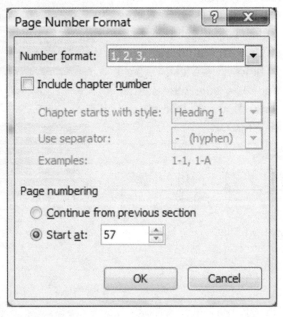

Click **OK** and the new document will start with the specified page number, **57** in this example; obviously the page numbers which follow are automatically incremented by Word, as required.

Inserting a Text Box in a Document

To emphasise a piece of text, you can enclose it within a border and set the text against a background. A simple method is to click the **Insert** tab and then **Text Box** off the Word ribbon in the **Text** group. A drop-down menu entitled **Built-In** appears offering a choice of different box formats. Ignore these and click **Draw Text Box** at the bottom. This provides a cross hair cursor which can be dragged out to give a rectangle of a suitable size, as shown below.

Now enter the text in the text box, applying any formatting in the usual way. The text box can be moved about the page by dragging. Alternatively hold down the **Ctrl** key and press the appropriate arrow key.

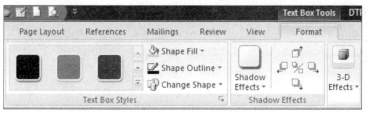

Borders and Shading

Select the text box so that the eight handles appear as shown in the empty text box above. Then click the **Format** tab on the ribbon. Numerous tools appear on the ribbon under **Text Box Tools**. **Shape Fill**, **Shape Outline** and **Change Shape** were used in the text box above.

Page Layout	References	Mailings	Review	View	Format

Shape Fill
Shape Outline
Change Shape

Text Box Styles

Shadow Effects

Shadow Effects

3-D Effects

Text Box Tools   DTP

Inserting Pictures into a Document

It's very useful to be able to insert pictures to enhance or illustrate the text, whether you're writing a letter, a report or magazine – or a technical or educational book such as this one.

Sourcing Your Pictures

Pictures may come from various sources; you may wish to draw on the libraries of *clip art* available for down-loading from the Internet. These are ready-made sketches and pictures and there are some available on your hard disc if you have installed Microsoft Word. Another source of images is the digital camera; images which you have taken yourself can be copied to your hard disc and then installed in a Word document. Similarly any existing photographic prints and pictures on paper can be scanned into your computer and saved on your hard disc. These topics are discussed in more detail in our book Digital Photography and Computing for the Older Generation from Bernard Babani Publishing Ltd.

The Internet is a rich source of images which can be captured and saved. However, you need to get permission from the owner of the copyright, especially if you intend to reproduce the image in any commercial application. Some professional photographers display their images for sale on their own Web site.

Capturing a Picture from a Web Page

I recently needed a picture of a steam train. Entering **steam train** into Google lead to various Web sites including the **ArtOriginals** site. This displayed lots of suitable pictures and a facility to contact the photographer.

After obtaining permission for the photographer, Bruce Malcolm it was simply a case of right-clicking over the required picture on the Web page and selecting **Save Picture As...** from the drop-down menu which appears. The **Save Picture** dialogue box appears as shown below.

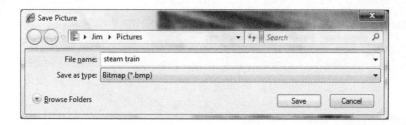

Make sure the required folder is selected in the address bar as shown above and enter a name, e.g **steam train**, in the **File name** bar and then click **Save**.

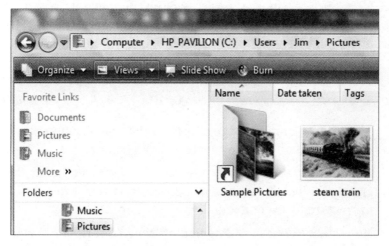

In this case the picture has been saved in the user's **Pictures** folder with the path **C:\Users\Jim\Pictures**.

The picture of a steam train is now saved on the hard disc in a known location. The full path to the photo, saved as a file with the name **steam train**, is:

C:\Users\Jim\Pictures\steam train

Now place the cursor on the page where the picture is to be inserted. From the Word ribbon, click the **Insert** tab and then click **Picture** from the **Illustrations** group.

Now browse in the **Insert Picture** dialogue box which appears, to find the folder where you have stored your picture. The correct path needs to appear in the address bar as shown in the example below.

Select the required image and click the **Insert** button at the bottom right of the **Insert Picture** dialogue box.

The picture should now be partially displayed, with the eight grab handles around its perimeter. (If necessary, click the picture to select it and display the handles).

Now click **Format** and **Position** off the Word ribbon. Select the required position of the picture from the menu as shown in the extract on the next page.

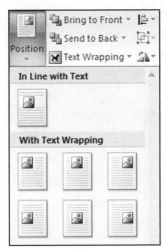

If you click over the picture to select it, eight "handles" are displayed, as shown below. Now you can move the picture to any position you like. Simply keep the left mouse button held down and drag the image about the page. Alternatively hold down the **Ctrl** key and use an arrow key to precisely nudge the picture into position. With the picture selected there are many other tools on the **Format** tab on the ribbon, including text wrapping and borders and shading.

Photo by Bruce Malcolm of fotosouvenirs

Inserting Clip Art into a Document

Enter the clip art library by clicking the **Insert** tab and then the **Clip Art** icon on the Word ribbon, as shown below.

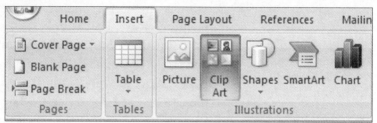

Now click **Organize clips...** from the small menu which appears at the bottom of the **Clip Art** pane on the right of the screen.   Double-click **Office Collections** on the left-hand side of the screen to

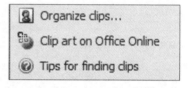

open up a library of clip art in various categories under **Collection List...** shown below. Further clip art is available from the Internet after clicking **Clips Online** shown below.

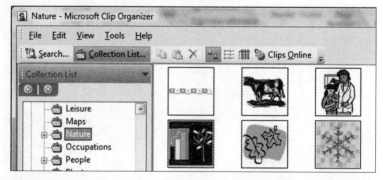

Select a picture then click **Edit** and **Copy**. Then click **Paste** off the **Home** tab on the Word ribbon. Now select the picture and click **Position** off the **Format** menu. You can move the picture about as just described for the train image.

Inserting Screenshots into a Document

It's often useful to be able to copy all or part of the screen for insertion into a document. For example, to copy some information from a Web site; or to illustrate some notes explaining how to use a piece of software. Most of the images in this book have been obtained in this way.

With the correct screen being displayed, press the **Prt Sc** key; this places a copy of the screen on the computer's clipboard, a temporary storage area. Now with the Word document open at the correct page, place the cursor where you want the top left-hand corner of the image to be. From the **Home** tab on the Word ribbon, click the **Paste** icon. An incomplete outline of the image appears on the page. Now click over the image to select it and click the **Format** tab on the ribbon. Click **Position** off the ribbon and then select one of the positions shown on the drop-down menu which appears. The image of the full screen appears as shown below.

Manipulating Screenshots and Other Images

Click over the image (screenshot, photo, picture, etc.) to select it so that the eight handles are visible. Now move it around by dragging with the mouse, continually holding down the left-hand button. Alternatively select the image then hold down the **Ctrl** key and press an arrow key to nudge the image accurately into position.

Resizing an Image in Word

The entire image can be enlarged or made smaller by dragging the small arrow heads which appear when you allow the cursor to hover over a corner of the image.

Cropping an Image in Word

If you only want to include part of an image, Word has a crop tool on the **Format** tab of the ribbon. Select the image then select the **Crop** icon. The image now has straight and right- angled crop tools around its perimeter, as shown below. These can be moved inwards to remove unwanted areas of the image, as shown below.

Click outside of the image to switch off the cropping tools and then enlarge the cropped image if necessary.

Saving a Document

All saving of the documents you produce should generally use the **Word Document (*.docx)** file format selected from the **Save as type** drop-down menu shown below, in the **Save As** dialogue box.

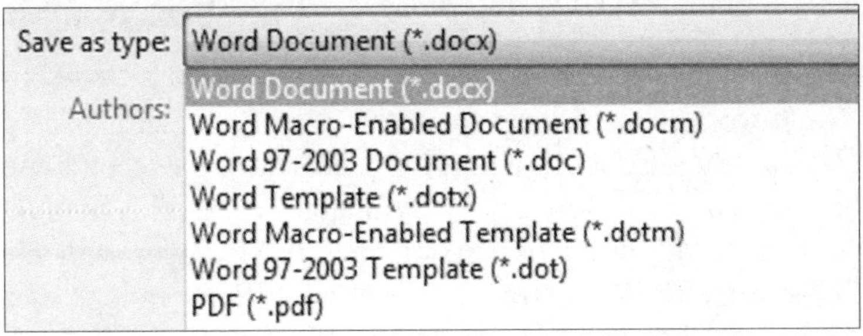

Save as type:	Word Document (*.docx)
Authors:	Word Document (*.docx)
	Word Macro-Enabled Document (*.docm)
	Word 97-2003 Document (*.doc)
	Word Template (*.dotx)
	Word Macro-Enabled Template (*.dotm)
	Word 97-2003 Template (*.dot)
	PDF (*.pdf)

Opening a Document in Earlier Versions of Word

It may be necessary to transfer a document to another computer after saving it on a CD or flash drive, or e-mailing it to a friend or colleague, for example. If the second computer uses an earlier version of Word it will not normally be able to open documents saved in the Word 2007 file format **Word Document (*.docx)**. To enable a Word 2007 document to be opened in earlier versions of Word, save it in the **Word 97-2003 Document (*.doc)** file format shown above. Alternatively, special software is available to enable earlier versions of Word to read files in the Word 2007 ***.docx** format.

When you save a copy of a Word document using **Save As** you specify the file name, the file type and the location on your hard disc or removable media. If you intend to keep the same file name, etc., as you keep adding to the document, there is a quick way to save the document, as discussed on the next page.

As you continue to work on the document, you can save the latest copy of the document by simply clicking on the disc icon on the **Quick Access Toolbar**.

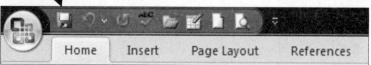

While working on a long document it's a good idea to keep clicking the disc icon regularly; it only takes a second and ensures you can't lose a lot of valuable work. This method overwrites the previous version of the document with the latest version; if you want to keep all of the versions of a document, then use **Save As** and enter a new file name each time you save.

As an extra safety measure, you can set the **AutoRecover** feature in Word. This automatically saves the data in a document every so often; this is useful if there is a power cut and you've forgotten to save your work at regular intervals as recommended above.

To set the **AutoRecover** feature, from the **Save As** dialogue box, select **Tools** and **Save Options**....

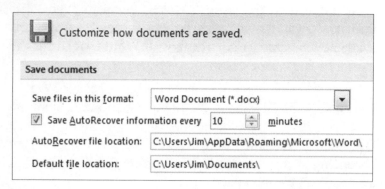

In the **Word Options** dialogue box shown on the previous page, click the check box to switch on **Save AutoRecover information every** and set a time in minutes. Click **OK**.

If there is a power cut or sudden computer problem, most of your work will have already been saved. When you start up again, Word displays the recovered document.

Making Backup Copies

It's possible to lose a document on a hard disc due to a technical problem or accidental deletion. When working on a long document such as a book, report or magazine it's essential to make regular backup copies on a separate medium such as a CD/DVD or USB flash drive or "dongle". These media are very cheap and can prevent you from losing many hours of work. My own preferred method is to make daily backups onto USB dongles. Then when a chapter is complete I make a more permanent backup onto a CD-R. This method is fast, simple and, so far, 100% reliable. To save onto a USB flash drive or a CD, in the **Save As** dialogue box click **Computer** (or **My Computer**) then double-click the removable medium. **Removable Disk (G:)** shown below is a USB flash drive.

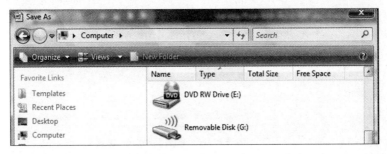

Now click the **Save** button to place a copy of the document on the removable medium such as a flash drive or CD.

Portable Document Format (PDF) Files

This is a format for saving files so that they can be opened and read on many different incompatible computer systems. Large organizations, such as government departments, etc., make many documents available for downloading from the Internet. These are normally created in the PDF format. To view a PDF file, all you need is a program called Adobe Reader, which can be downloaded free from the Internet at **www.adobe.com/uk**.

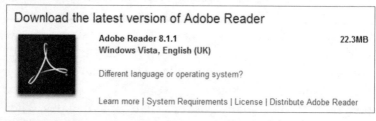

If you are intending to have a document such as a magazine or book printed and published, it's a good idea to be able to save it on a CD/DVD in PDF format. This is because the printers or publishers may not use equipment compatible with Word 2007 or Windows PC computers; however, they will almost certainly be able to handle PDF files.

At one time it was necessary to use a special program such as Adobe Acrobat to create files in the PDF format; Word 2007 has its own option to create PDF files, in the **Save as type** menu in the **Save As** dialogue box shown below.

Save as type:	PDF (*.pdf)
Authors:	Word Document (*.docx) Word Macro-Enabled Document (*.docm) Word 97-2003 Document (*.doc)
Optimize for:	Word Template (*.dotx) Word Macro-Enabled Template (*.dotm) Word 97-2003 Template (*.dot)
	PDF (*.pdf)

Shown below are two pages of this chapter saved using the PDF option in Word 2007 and opened in Adobe Reader.

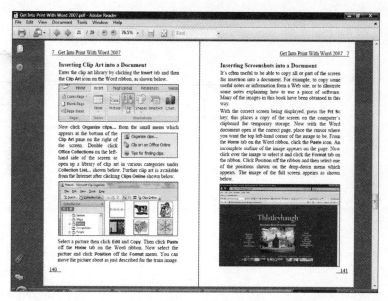

You will normally find that the **PDF** file is a faithful copy of the original Word document. If you do find any discrepancies, you will not be able to carry out any major editing in Adobe Reader – this is essentially a viewer, as shown by the menu bar below. Although there is an **Edit** menu, this does not allow you to delete or insert text, etc.

If a document in PDF format needs editing, you must return to the original Word document in **.doc.x** or **.doc** format, then resave it as a new PDF file.

Mailshots and Labels the Easy Way

Introduction

I've often been asked to help with the printing of letters and address labels for mailings to a large number of people. The topics in this chapter should be useful to anyone sending out a lot of correspondence, for example:

- The secretary of a club, group or society
- An administrator in a business sending out invoices, advertisements, etc., to customers/clients
- Anyone sending out a lot of invitations, greetings or Christmas cards, etc.

Once you've created a file containing all of the records, you can use it over and over again – there's no need to spend hours retyping or handwriting the names and addresses. The mailing list can also be used selectively – you can specify which people in the address file are to receive a particular mailing.

Creating a Mailshot – an Overview

This involves sending the same basic letter to many different people; each copy of the letter is personalized for individual recipients, so that one letter might start "Dear Mike" while another would begin "Dear Jill", together with their corresponding addresses.

There are two main components of the mailshot:

- The basic skeleton of the letter which is the same for everyone

- A list of names and addresses saved as a separate file, often referred to as the *data source.*

The list of names and addresses is first created and saved as a separate file, for example in Excel 2007 or Access 2007.

It's very easy and efficient to create an address file in Excel 2007; for example, I have used Excel with a mailing list for a society with several hundred members.

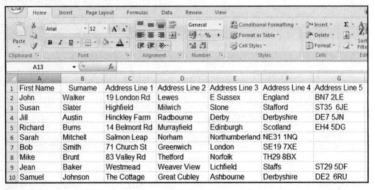

Excel 2007, which is supplied as part of Office 2007, is used as the data source for the examples which follow in the remainder of this chapter.

After creating the Excel file, the basic letter is then typed in Word 2007, including a set of *placeholders* or *mail merge fields.* These are marked locations in the standard letter into which the individual names and addresses will be placed.

The mail merge then takes place, during which individual names and addresses are copied from the Excel file into each unique copy of the letter. Finally the individual letters are printed.

Creating the Address File in Excel 2007

From **Start**, **All Programs** and **Microsoft Office**, select **Microsoft Office Excel 2007** as shown below.

After you've used Excel the first time it can subsequently be launched directly from the main **Start** menu.

Excel opens ready for you to start entering the column headings, such as **First Name**, **Surname**, **Address Line 1**, **Address Line 2**, etc., as shown in the extract below.

	A	B	C	D	E
1	First Name	Surname	Address Line 1	Address Line 2	Address Line 3
2	John	Walker	19 London Rd	Lewes	E Sussex
3	Susan	Slater	Highfield	Milwich	Stone
4	Jill	Austin	Hinckley Farm	Radbourne	Derby
5	Richard	Burns	14 Belmont Rd	Murrayfield	Edinburgh
6	Sarah	Mitchell	Salmon Leap	Norham	Northumberland
7	Bob	Smith	71 Church St	Greenwich	London
8	Mike	Brunt	83 Valley Rd	Thetford	Norfolk

The column headings **First Name**, **Surname**, etc., play a crucial part in the mail merge, as will be seen later.

Entering the Data

It's simply a case of typing the names and addresses into the cells. *Don't use commas or punctuation marks* within an address field; "83, Valley Rd", for example, might cause problems. To move to a new cell press the **Enter** key to move down and the **Tab** key to move across.

You'll probably need to extend the width of the columns to accommodate the column titles and also the data. To do this, allow the cursor to dwell between the column headers. The cursor changes to a small cross, shown between **D** and **E** below. The cross can then be dragged to give the correct column width, while holding down the left mouse button.

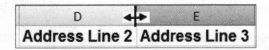

Text can be formatted in the cells in Excel in a similar way to text in a word processor; the ribbon in Excel contains the usual text formatting tools, as shown below.

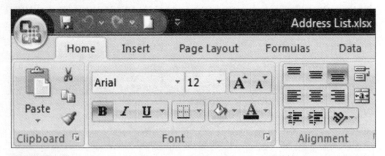

To edit the data in a cell, first double-click the cell. To carry out formatting of an entire row or column, first click the row or column header cell (**1,2,3**, etc., and **A, B, C**, etc.,) to select the row or column.

Saving the Excel File of Names and Addresses

Click the **Office Button** in the top left-hand corner of Excel and select **Save As** from the drop-down menu. The file is saved as an Excel Workbook with the file name **Address List.xlsx** in this example, entered in the **File name** slot, as shown below.

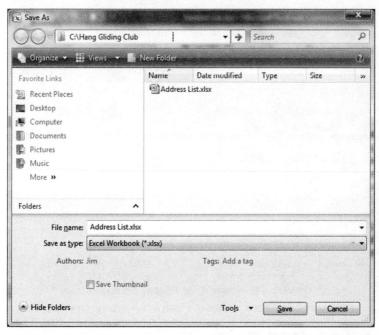

Make a note of the location where the address file is saved; you will need to browse for this file shortly when you carry out the mail merge in Word 2007. In this example I have used the **New Folder** option, shown above on the **Save As** menu bar, to create a folder **Hang Gliding Club**. The full path to the data source for the mail merge is therefore:

C:\Hang Gliding Club\Address List.xlsx

Creating the Skeleton Letter

The letter is typed in Word 2007 in the usual way, leaving space for the recipient's name and address and also a space for their name in the greeting as in Dear *****.

High Peak Hang Gliding Club
Roaches House
Leek
Staffordshire
ST6 5BY

29 June 2008

Space for recipient's

name and address

Dear | *Name*

National Over 50s Hang Gliding Championship

This year we will again be fielding a team in this prestigious event; if you would like to be considered for selection, please reply to me by letter at the above address, as soon as possible.

The next task is to add the placeholders or mail merge fields to the skeleton letter; the placeholders mark the positions where the names and addresses are to be inserted.

With the skeleton letter open in Word 2007, select the **Mailings** tab from the ribbon, then select **Start Mail Merge** and **Step by Step Mail Merge Wizard...** from the drop-down menu which appears.

In the right-hand panel of the wizard, under **Select document type**, make sure the radio button next to **Letters** is switched on. Then select **Next: Starting document** at the bottom of the right-hand panel.

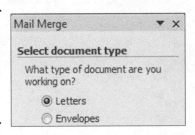

Under **Select starting document** select **Use the current document** and then select **Next: Select recipients** at the bottom of the right-hand panel.

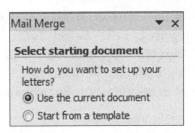

Make sure **Use an existing list** is selected in the right-hand panel and then click **Browse...** shown on the right below. The **Select Data Source** window opens, allowing you to search the folders on your hard disc to find the file of names and addresses. In the previous example, the file of names and addresses **Address List.xlsx**

was stored in the **Hang Gliding Club** folder shown below in the **Select Data Source** window.

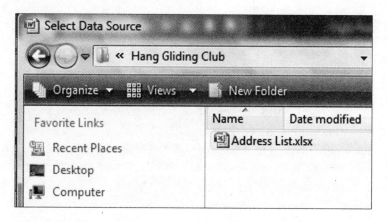

Now click the name of the required file **Address List.xlsx** in this example and click the **Open** button. A small window opens entitled **Select Table**. You will probably only use **Sheet1$** in Excel for your address file so leave this highlighted and make sure the check box against **First row of data contains column headers** is ticked.

Click **OK** and you are presented with your list of names and addresses in the **Mail Merge Recipients** window shown in the small extract below.

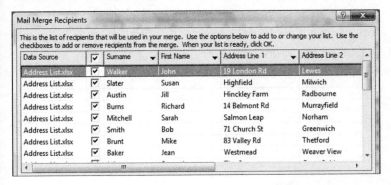

The check boxes against each name can be used to remove a recipient from the list or add someone if they have been omitted from an earlier mailing.

Click **OK** and then click **Next: Write your** letter at the bottom right of the **Mail Merge** panel. Then you can write your letter if you've not already done so. In this example we have already written the skeleton letter so we go straight on to inserting the placeholders for the names and addresses.

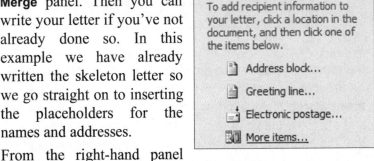

From the right-hand panel select **More items...** as shown on the right.

Inserting the Placeholders or Merge Fields

The **Insert Merge Field** window opens as shown below; under **Fields** you can see that the Word 2007 mail merge facility has imported the column headings from across the top of the Excel spreadsheet, i.e. **First Name**, **Surname**, **Address Line 1**, etc.

We now need to insert these placeholders or merge fields in the required positions in the skeleton letter. Place the cursor on the letter where the **First Name** is to appear and from the **Insert Merge Field** window shown above, select **First Name** and click the **Insert** button. The words **First Name** appear in the skeleton letter at the current cursor position, and are surrounded in chevrons as shown below.

«First_Name»

Now move the cursor to the position in the letter for the next placeholder i.e. the surname, and click **More items...**, click **Surname** in the **Insert Merge Field** window and click **Insert** shown to place the **Surname** merge field on the letter. Continue with this method until you have inserted all of the required placeholders.

Alternatively you might choose to insert all of your place holders first, without changing the cursor position and clicking **More items....** Then you could cut and paste the placeholders into the required layout.

High Peak Hang Gliding Club
Roaches House
Leek
Staffordshire
ST6 5BY

29 June 2008

«First_Name» «Surname»
«Address_Line_1»
«Address_Line_2»
«Address_Line_3»
«Address_Line_4»
«Address_Line_5»

Dear «First_Name»

National Over 50s Hang Gliding Championship

This year we will again be fielding a team in this prestigious event; if you would like to be considered for selection, please reply to me by letter at the above address, as soon as possible.

Please note that each of the placeholders or merge fields within chevrons, such as **«Surname»**, can be moved, edited or deleted to give the required layout. For example, you could move two merge fields together as shown above in:

«First_Name» «Surname»

Infilling the Names and Addresses

When you are happy with the placeholders, click **Next: Preview your letters** at the bottom of the right-hand panel. Immediately the place holders are replaced by the actual name and address of the first person in your Excel file.

> High Peak Hang Gliding Club
> Roaches House
> Leek
> Staffordshire
> ST6 5BY
>
> 29 June 2008
>
> John Walker
> 19 London Rd
> Lewes
> E Sussex
> England BN7 2LE|
>
> Dear John
>
> **National Over 50s Hang Gliding Championship**
> This year we will again be fielding a team in this prestigious event; if you

The **Mail Merge** panel now allows you to preview your letters one at a time. You can also **Edit recipient list...** as discussed earlier in this chapter and also remove the recipient currently displayed in the letter on the screen.

Finally **Next: Complete the merge** is selected and then **Print...** to print all of your letters on paper, including the individual names, addresses and greetings.

Mail Merge ▼ ×

Preview your letters

One of the merged letters is previewed here. To preview another letter, click one of the following:

[<<] Recipient: 1 [>>]

🔍 Find a recipient...

Make changes

You can also change your recipient list:

📝 Edit recipient list...

[Exclude this recipient]

Printing Address Labels

Once you've created your Excel file of names and addresses, it can also be used to print address labels to stick on envelopes and parcels. These could be used for sending out club or society newsletters, invoices or Christmas cards for example. This can save many hours of work; the Excel file may need to be edited from time to time as people move away or newcomers need to be added.

The method for printing labels is very similar to that just described for infilling names and addresses into a standard letter. The main features of this method are:

- The file of names and addresses created in Excel
- The Mail Merge Wizard in Word 2007
- Sheets of sticky labels in a specified format.

The sheets of sticky labels can be bought from stationers; many labels are supplied on a grid on A4 backing paper which can be used in a standard laser, inkjet or dot-matrix printer. There are many different manufacturers of labels; for example, you might choose one of the Avery A4 range.

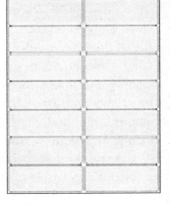

The Avery template L7163 provides 14 labels per A4 sheet, as shown on the right. The template number L7163 is specified during the Mail Merge Wizard and your names and addresses are printed to match this layout. It's a good idea to print some "labels" on ordinary A4 paper as a test, before using the actual sticky labels.

Although the printing of labels has much in common with the mail merge letter just described, the printing of labels is described here in full so that it can be read independently. However, the same Excel address file is used as the data source for the labels and the creation of this is not repeated.

From the **Mailings** tab select **Start Mail Merge** and **Step by Step Mail Merge Wizard**....

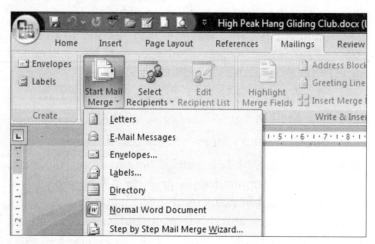

From the **Mail Merge** panel which appears on the right-hand side of the screen, select **Labels**. Now select **Next: Starting document** at the bottom right of the screen and then click **Label options...** under **Change document layout** in the centre of the right-hand panel. The **Label Options** window opens as shown on the next a page.

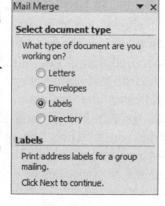

Choosing a Label Specification

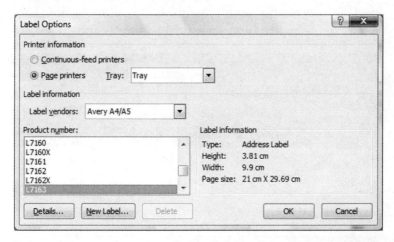

Select the manufacturer of your labels from the drop-down menu next to **Label vendors** and then scroll down and select your particular labels under **Product number** shown above. Click the **OK** button and then click **Next: Select recipients** from the bottom of the right-hand panel.

Selecting the Recipients

From the right-hand panel, since we are using an existing Excel file, make sure **Use an existing list** is selected and then click **Browse...**, shown below on the right. This enables you to search your hard disc or other storage device such as a flash drive or dongle to find the Excel file containing your names and addresses.

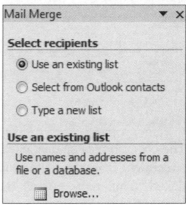

The **Select Data Source** window opens, from which you can browse through your hard disc, etc., using the Computer/Windows Explorer type feature as shown below.

Now select the name of the required file (**Address List.xlsx** in this example) and click the **Open** button. The **Select Table** window opens; make sure **Sheet1$ is** highlighted and that there is a tick against **First row of data contains column headers**. Click **OK** and you are presented with your list of names and addresses in the **Mail Merge Recipients** window shown in the small extract below.

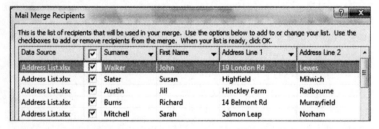

The check boxes against each name can be used to remove a recipient from the list or add someone whose name is not ticked. This only affects the current mailing – not the contents of the original Excel file used as the data source.

Arranging the Placeholders or Merge Fields

Now select **Next: Arrange your labels** and click **More items...** in the right-hand panel, as shown on the right. The **Insert Merge Field** window opens as shown below. Select the first field, **First Name** in this example, and click **Insert** to place it on the Word page as a placeholder or merge field.

Mail Merge   ▼ ✕

Arrange your labels

If you have not already done so, lay out your label using the first label on the sheet.

To add recipient information to your label, click a location in the first label, and then click one of the items below.

📄 Address block...

📄 Greeting line...

📑 Electronic postage...

🗐 More items...

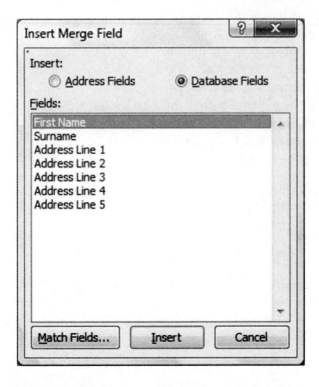

Insert Merge Field   ? ✕

Insert:
   ○ Address Fields   ● Database Fields

Fields:

First Name
Surname
Address Line 1
Address Line 2
Address Line 3
Address Line 4
Address Line 5

Match Fields...   Insert   Cancel

Continue highlighting and inserting the placeholders onto the page. Don't worry about the layout until all the placeholders are on the Word page. You can select the place holders and cut and paste them to move them about into your chosen layout for the labels.

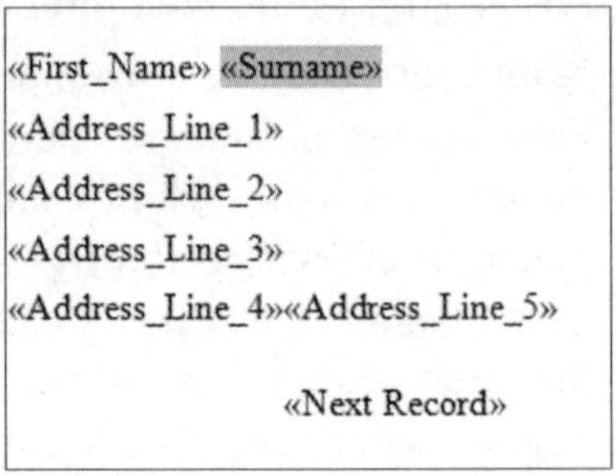

«First_Name» «Surname»

«Address_Line_1»

«Address_Line_2»

«Address_Line_3»

«Address_Line_4»«Address_Line_5»

«Next Record»

Now select **Update all labels**, shown on the right. This will take your layout for the placeholders and apply it to every other label in the mailing. As shown in the small extract below, at this stage there are no actual names or addresses – it's just a grid of placeholders. The next stage is to infill the actual data from the Excel file.

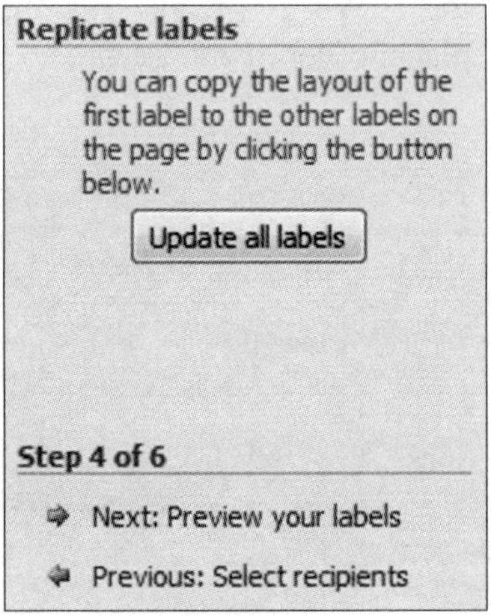

Replicate labels

You can copy the layout of the first label to the other labels on the page by clicking the button below.

Update all labels

Step 4 of 6

➡ Next: Preview your labels

⬅ Previous: Select recipients

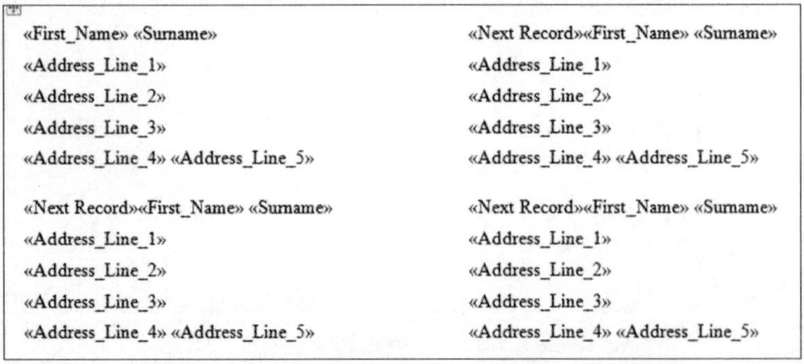

«First_Name» «Surname»	«Next Record»«First_Name» «Surname»
«Address_Line_1»	«Address_Line_1»
«Address_Line_2»	«Address_Line_2»
«Address_Line_3»	«Address_Line_3»
«Address_Line_4» «Address_Line_5»	«Address_Line_4» «Address_Line_5»
«Next Record»«First_Name» «Surname»	«Next Record»«First_Name» «Surname»
«Address_Line_1»	«Address_Line_1»
«Address_Line_2»	«Address_Line_2»
«Address_Line_3»	«Address_Line_3»
«Address_Line_4» «Address_Line_5»	«Address_Line_4» «Address_Line_5»

To check that the all of the names and addresses from the Excel file are present and correct, select **Next: Preview your labels** from the bottom of the **Mail Merge** panel. The first batch of labels is shown on the screen in the layout determined by your chosen brand and size of sticky labels. In the label format shown below, each A4 sheet has 21 labels arranged in 3 columns and 7 rows.

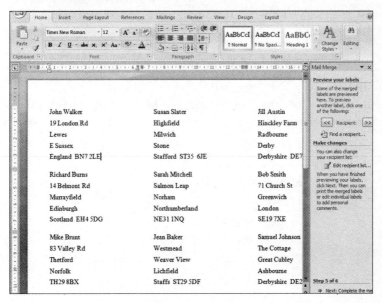

In the right-hand panel shown above and on the right, you can scroll through the recipients and edit individual labels; you can also return to the mailing list and make changes after selecting **Edit recipient list**....

Finally select **Next: Complete the merge** from the bottom of the right-hand panel. You are now ready to print the labels by clicking **Print...** as shown on the lower right. You may wish to carry out a "dummy run" using ordinary A4 paper before adding the actual label stationery to your printer.

After clicking **Print...**, the **Merge to Printer** window appears, allowing you to specify how many of the labels are to be printed.

Future Mailshots and Label Printing

With all of your names and addresses saved in an Excel file on the hard disc, you can use the list over and over again for mailshots for different purposes. Simply make sure the required recipients are ticked in the **Mail Merge Recipients** window shown earlier in this chapter. Alternatively you might create different Excel files as the data sources for different purposes such as business or social.

Middle-Aged Spreadsheets

Introduction

Many of us who've reached middle-age and beyond are constantly encouraged to watch our weight in order to maintain (or regain) a healthy lifestyle. One of the indicators used to measure the success or otherwise of our efforts is the Body Mass Index or BMI. This is calculated from the formula:-

$$BMI = \frac{\text{Weight in Kilograms}}{\text{(Height in Metres) x (Height in Metres)}}$$

Unfortunately the "older generation" grew up with Imperial units – feet and inches and stones and pounds; many of us are still reluctant to use the new metric units, even though, it has to be conceded, they are much simpler to work with in certain situations, as this chapter will show.

This chapter shows how to calculate the Body Mass Index for a group of people such as a fitness club or group of friends and to draw a chart enabling comparisons to be made. The work is based on the Excel 2007 spreadsheet program and will describe how BMI can be calculated using both metric and Imperial units as the raw data.

Creating the Spreadsheet – Metric Version

From **Start**, **All Programs** and **Microsoft Office**, select **Microsoft Office Excel 2007**.

After you've used Excel the first time, in future it can be launched directly from the main **Start** menu.

We will initially set up a spreadsheet based on height in metres and weight in kilograms, as this is simpler. If you are not happy working in these metric units, the work is repeated shortly using feet and inches and stones and pounds.

First we need to enter the labels for the rows and columns, such as **Height**, etc., and **Mike**, etc., as shown below.

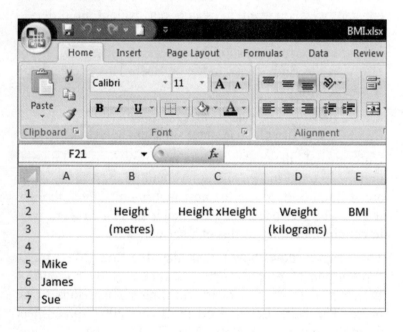

If you want to apply formatting such as centring, just click in the header at the beginning of the row or column, either **1**, **2**, **3**, etc., or **A**, **B**, **C**, etc., on the previous screenshot. To widen column **C** to accommodate the title **Height x Height**, place the cursor on the line between **C** and **D**. Then drag the small cross which appears until the column is the correct width.

Entering the Data

Enter the **Height** in metres and **Weight** in kilograms for each person.

	A	B	C	D	E
1					
2		Height	Height xHeight	Weight	BMI
3		(metres)		(kilograms)	
4					
5	Mike	1.83		108.41	
6	James	1.75		88.00	
7	Sue	1.57		52.16	
8	Jill	1.63		60.33	

Formatting Numbers to Two Decimal Places

In the above example the numbers in the two columns have been formatted to two decimal places by clicking in the header at the top of each column. Then from the Excel ribbon with the **Home** tab selected, click the arrow to the right of **General** under **View**. Now select **Number** from the drop-down menu shown on the right.

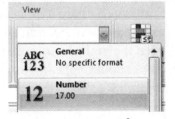

We now need to calculate **Height x Height** or **(Height)^2**

	A	B	C	D	E
				f_x =B5*B5	
1					
2		Height	Height xHeight	Weight	BMI
3		(metres)		(kilograms)	
4					
5	Mike	1.83	=B5*B5	108.41	
6	James	1.75		88.00	

Place the cursor in cell **C5** and type an equals (**=**) sign. This signifies that the cell will contain a formula. We need to multiply the number in cell **B5** by itself, i.e. **B5 x B5**. However, in spreadsheet work ***** is used as the multiplication sign. So click cell **B5**, type the ***** sign in cell **C5** and click cell **B5** again to complete the formula. Alternatively you can simply type the formula directly into cell **C5**. Please also note that formulas can be edited in the formula bar across the top of the spreadsheet.

When you are satisfied the formula is correct, click the tick shown in the formula bar at the top of the spreadsheet. Now the answer, **3.35**, not the formula, appears in cell **C5**.

Replication

This is the easy bit. Now we've set up the formula **B5*B5** in cell **C5** we need to go all the way down column **C**, replicating the formula so that we have **B6*B6**, **B7*B7**, etc. Fortunately there's no need to laboriously enter all of these formulas down column **C**. Simply allow the cursor to hover over the right-hand bottom corner of cell **C5** and a small cross should appear. Now drag this cross all the way down column **C** as shown on the next page.

		f_x	=B5*B5	

	A	B	C	D	E
1					
2		Height	Height xHeight	Weight	BMI
3		(metres)		(kilograms)	
4					
5	Mike	1.83	3.35	108.41	
6	James	1.75		88.00	
7	Sue	1.57	Drag the small cross	52.16	
8	Jill	1.63	down column to replicate the formula	60.33	
9	Pat	1.65	in cells C6, C7, C8,	64.41	
10	Tom	1.73	etc.	69.40	

You will see that all of the cells are automatically filled in with calculated answers for **Height*Height**. This method of replication can be used for formulas both down columns and along rows; on a large spreadsheet with more complex formulas it can save many hours of work.

Calculating the Body Mass Index

We now need to place the cursor in cell **E5** to calculate the first **BMI**. We have to divide the **Weight** in **D5** by the **Height x Height** in **C5**. Spreadsheets use the forward slash **/** for division, so the formula to be entered in cell **E5** is **=D5/C5**.

		X ✓ f_x	=D5/C5	

	A	B	C	D	E
1					
2		Height	Height xHeight	Weight	BMI
3		(metres)		(kilograms)	
4					
5	Mike	1.83	3.35	108.41	=D5/C5
6	James	1.75	3.06	88.00	

It's now just a case of clicking the tick in the entry bar and dragging the small cross down column **E**, as previously discussed, to replicate the formulas. The Body Mass Indices based on metric measurements for 10 entirely fictitious people is shown below.

	A	B	C	D	E
				f_x	
1					
2		Height	Height xHeight	Weight	BMI
3		(metres)		(kilograms)	
4					
5	Mike	1.83	3.35	108.41	32.37
6	James	1.75	3.06	88.00	28.73
7	Sue	1.57	2.46	52.16	21.16
8	Jill	1.63	2.66	60.33	22.71
9	Pat	1.65	2.72	64.41	23.66
10	Tom	1.73	2.99	69.40	23.19
11	Mac	1.85	3.42	62.60	18.29
12	David	1.78	3.17	109.32	34.50
13	Stella	1.60	2.56	70.76	27.64
14	Richard	1.78	3.17	78.47	24.77
15					

It's often easier to interpret tables of figures using graphs and charts and this is discussed shortly.

The next task is to create the same spreadsheet using Imperial units as the raw data and this is described on the pages which follow.

Creating the Spreadsheet Using Imperial Units

The next section shows how the heights can be entered in feet and inches and converted automatically to metres. Similarly the weights will be entered in stones and pounds and converted to kilograms.

Converting Feet and Inches to Metres

The extract below shows the new column headings to accommodate the height in feet and inches.

	A	B	C	D	E	F
1						
2		Height		Height	Height	Height xHeight
3		feet	inches	ins	metres	
4						
5	Mike	6	0	72	1.83	3.34
6	James	5	9	69	1.75	3.07

The label **Height** above is spread across two selected cells by selecting **Merge Cells** from the **Alignment** group on the **Home** tab of the Excel ribbon, shown on the right.

The feet and inches are entered in two separate columns; the height is converted to inches by the formula **=B5*12+C5**. This formula is entered in cell **D5**, where the answer appears. The formula is then replicated down column **D**, to give **=B6*12+C6, =B7*12+C7**, etc.

The height in metres (column **E**) is obtained by multiplying the height in inches (column **D**) by **0.0254**. On the spreadsheet this is achieved by entering the formula **=D5*0.0254** into cell **E5**, where the answer is to appear. Column **E** is completed by replication as previously described.

Converting Stones and Pounds to Kilograms

F	G	H	I	J	K
Height xHeight	Weight		Weight	Weight	BMI
	stones	pounds	pounds	kilograms	
3.34	17	1	239	108.41	32.41
3.07	13	12	194	88.00	28.65

The weight in pounds is calculated by entering the formula =**G5*14+H5** in cell **I5**. This formula can then be replicated down column **I** as previously discussed. To obtain the weight in kilograms, multiply the weight in pounds by **0.4536**. This is done by entering the formula = **I5*0.4536** in cell **J5**. Then the weights in kilograms are completed by replication down column **J** as previously discussed.

To convert the numbers in a column to a more manageable 2 decimal places, click the column header to select the column, then select **Number** under **View** on the Excel **Home** tab as described earlier.

We now have the heights in metres and the weights in kilograms as in the metric version of the spreadsheet as discussed earlier in this chapter.

It's now just a case of multiplying (height x height), **E5*E5** and placing the answer in **F5**. Then replicate this formula down column **F**.

Finally the BMI column is completed by dividing weight in kilograms by (height x height), as before. This is achieved by entering the formula =**J5/F5** in cell **K5** and this is replicated down column **K** as discussed earlier.

The completed BMI spreadsheet in Imperial units is shown below. The calculated cells are displayed to two decimal places after selecting **Number** from the Excel **Home** tab.

	F19	▾		f_x						
	A	B	C	D	E	F	G	H	I	J	K
1											
2		Height		Height	Height	Height xHeight	Weight		Weight	Weight	BMI
3		feet	inches	ins	metres		stones	pounds	pounds	kilograms	
4											
5	Mike	6	0	72	1.83	3.34	17	1	239	108.41	32.41
6	James	5	9	69	1.75	3.07	13	12	194	88.00	28.65
7	Sue	5	2	62	1.57	2.48	8	3	115	52.16	21.03
8	Jill	5	4	64	1.63	2.64	9	7	133	60.33	22.83
9	Sarah	5	5	65	1.65	2.73	14	3	199	90.27	33.12
10	Tom	5	8	68	1.73	2.98	10	13	153	69.40	23.26
11	Mac	6	1	73	1.85	3.44	9	12	138	62.60	18.21
12	Peter	5	10	70	1.78	3.16	17	3	241	109.32	34.58
13	Stella	5	3	63	1.60	2.56	11	2	156	70.76	27.63
14	Richard	5	10	70	1.78	3.16	12	5	173	78.47	24.82
15											

Recalculation – What if?

This is one of the most useful features of any spreadsheet and allows you make "what if?" speculations very easily. For example, Sarah's weight (14 stone 3 pounds) and BMI (**33.12**) is shown below.

14	3	199	90.27	33.12

What if Sarah reduced her weight to 10 stone 2 lbs?

Simply double-click each of the cells containing **14** and **3** and type in **10** and **2** instead. When you press **Enter** the new BMI (**23.63**) is automatically calculated and displayed instantly, as shown below.

10	2	142	64.41	23.63

Displaying Formulas

If your spreadsheet is not delivering the correct results and you want to check your calculations, you can display the *formulas* instead of the *data* in the cells.

To see all of the formulas in the cells of a spreadsheet, click the **Formulas** tab on the Excel ribbon and then click **Show Formulas** on the right-hand side of the ribbon, as shown right and below.

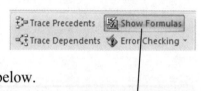

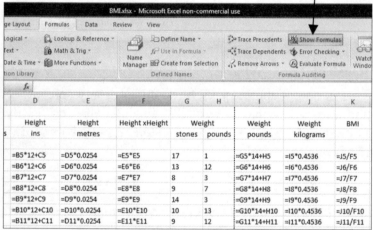

To revert back to the display of data, click **Show Formulas** on the ribbon again.

Save the spreadsheet by clicking **Save As** from the **Office Button**; the file is saved as an Excel Workbook with a name such as **BMI.xlsx**.

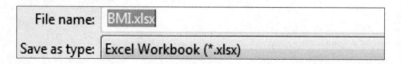

| File name: | BMI.xlsx |
| Save as type: | Excel Workbook (*.xlsx) |

Creating a Column Chart

Tables of figures can be difficult to interpret, whereas graphs and charts can usually be understood at a glance. For example, we could draw a column chart of the BMI for each person in the metric spreadsheet described earlier. The method for the Imperial spreadsheet is exactly the same. The chart will be based on data in the **Name** column and the data in the **BMI** column. First select the **Name** column by clicking in the header **A**. Next, while holding down the **Ctrl** key, click the header in the **BMI** column, **E** in the example below. Both the **Name** column and the **BMI** column should now be selected, as shown by the highlighting of the columns in the small extract below.

	A	B	C	D	E
1					
2	Name	Height	Height xHeight	Weight	BMI
3		(metres)		(kilograms)	
4					
5	Mike	1.83	3.35	108.41	32.37
6	James	1.75	3.06	88.00	28.73

Now click the **Insert** tab on the Excel ribbon and select the type of chart you want, from the many on offer in the drop-down menu, as shown in the small sample below.

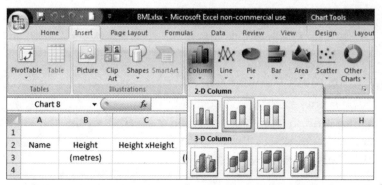

After you've selected the type of chart you want, the chart appears on the spreadsheet, as shown below.

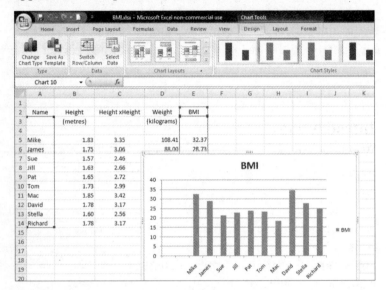

At this stage you can still change the type of chart by clicking the **Design** tab, and selecting **Change Chart Type** shown above. You can edit the title or label the horizontal and vertical axes after selecting the **Layout** tab on the ribbon and then clicking **Chart Title** or **Axis Titles**.

Saving and Printing a Chart

When you save a spreadsheet, using **Save As** from the **Office Button**, the chart is saved with it. To print the chart on its own, select the chart by clicking within its frame, then select **Print** from the **Office Button** menu.

8

Music While You Work

Introduction

Windows Vista includes the popular feature, Windows Media Player 11. Amongst other things, this allows you to create a library of your favourite music. In fact this latest version is capable of handling millions of music tracks so you could build an impressive library. You can choose from a long list of designs, known as *skins,* for the appearance of your virtual media player, such as the example shown below.

You can play video clips as with earlier versions of the Media Player. One major improvement with Windows Vista is that it is much easier to use DVDs. With the old Windows XP, it was necessary to buy additional software, such as Nero Ahead Software AG, if you wanted to record DVDs. It is now just a simple matter of inserting the disc into the player, without the need for special software.

As the Media Player uses both CDs and DVDs, it is useful to have one of the modern drives which combine both. These can be bought cheaply and simply slot into the computer, replacing the old CD drive.

Windows Media Player 11 is much more interactive with other modern portable devices, rather than being a 'stand-alone' player. Music, video and pictures can be copied onto mobile phones, digital cameras and MP3 players. This is very easy to do – just connect the device and easy-to-follow instructions will guide you.

A key difference of the latest Media Player is its ease of use. Navigation between menus has improved with 'back and forward' buttons – as found on the Internet screens. There is a greater emphasis on the use of helpful graphics, which were not provided on earlier versions. These include album covers and graphics showing available storage space.

URGE is a music network service which for a monthly subscription allows you to choose from millions of records and download them to your computer. The capacity to find music and store them in a library has never been so great.

Uses of the Windows Media Player

Windows Media Player 11 is far more versatile than a conventional music centre or video player. The following is a list of some of the things you can do with the Media Player:

- Play your favourite music in the background while working away at the computer.

- Copy music from CDs/DVDs to your hard disc (known as "ripping"), so that you no longer need to find and insert the disc.

- Organise and manage audio and video files by creating your own playlists in the **Library**.

- "Burn" your own audio CDs/DVDs by copying music from your hard disc.

- Download or "stream" (play directly) audio and video clips from the Internet.

- Copy music/video/pictures to a wide range of portable devices (e.g. mobile phones, pocket PCs, digital cameras). This is known as "media sharing".

- Use the **Instant Search** facility to find a particular track, artist or album title.

- Use the **URGE** network service to add music. There are over 2 million songs to choose from.

- Choose from a range of **Visualisations** – animated patterns which move in time with the music. An ample number of visualizations are supplied and you can download even more from the Internet.

- Change the styling of your on-screen media player using the **Skin Chooser**.

Starting to Use the Media Player

The Media Player is part of Windows Vista and can be launched from the **Start** orb, **All Programs** and **Windows Media Player**. (If you've not yet obtained Windows Vista, the media player is available separately).

The media player can also be started by placing an audio CD/DVD in the drive, then selecting **Play audio CD** as shown below in the **AutoPlay** window which appears.

The media player opens in its own window occupying the whole screen, as shown below. Across the top is a small menu bar with **File**, **View**, **Play**, **Tools** and **Help** drop-down menus. These only appear if you have switched on **Classic Menus**. (Right-click over the main menu bar and click **Show Classic Menus**). Below the Classic Menu bar are the main buttons which launch the various main features of the media player, namely **Now Playing**, **Library**, **Rip**, **Burn**, **Sync** and **Media Guide**.

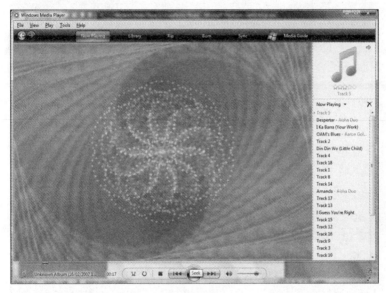

The Windows Media Player has the usual **Play**, **Pause**, **Stop, Previous** and **Next** buttons, etc., as shown below.

The two left-hand icons above are **Turn Shuffle On** and **Repeat**. On the right-hand side there is a **Mute** button and a **Volume Slider**.

Visualisations

Most of the **Now Playing** window shown on the previous page is occupied by a constantly changing artistic display, which moves in time with the music. This display is known as a **Visualization** and a large number of designs are available. You can change the design of the visualization by selecting **Now Playing**, then **Visualizations** in the drop-down menu as shown below.

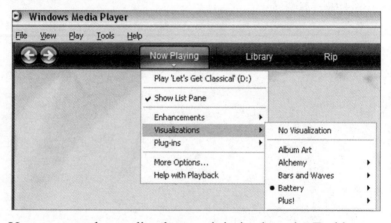

You can use the media player minimized on the Taskbar at the bottom of the screen, while freeing the screen for other tasks. Right-click over the Taskbar in an empty space, e.g. somewhere to the left of the time. From the menu which pops up click **Toolbars** and **Windows Media Player**. This is a one-off operation and will not need to be repeated. Whenever you minimize the Windows Media Player in future it will appear as the **Mini Player** on the Taskbar as shown below. There is a small **Restore** button on the extreme right at the bottom of the Mini Player to return the view to **Full Screen** mode.

Skin Mode

The media player can be switched between the **Full Mode** (shown previously) and the **Skin Mode** shown below. This is done by selecting **Skin Mode** from the **View** menu across the top of the media player window in **Full Mode**. Some skins are available directly from your hard disc after clicking **Skin Chooser**. Alternatively a vast array of highly creative skins can be downloaded from the Internet after clicking **More Skins**. Then click **Apply Skin** after you have chosen a design.

The Windows Media Player in **Skin Mode** has all the usual controls such as **Play**, **Pause**, **Stop**, etc. There are also options to return to full screen mode, to minimize the player on the Taskbar and to exit.

Copying Music from CDs to Your Computer

It's very convenient to make copies of your favourite CD tracks onto your hard disc. This means that the music you enjoy is always available while you are working at the computer. You don't have to search around for CDs and keep swapping them in the drive. You can also copy just a selection of your favourite tracks and it's possible to organize these into personalized playlists.

To begin the copy process, place the required CD in the drive and select **Rip** **music from CD** from the **AudioPlay** dialogue box which pops up, as shown earlier in this chapter.

Rip music from CD
using Windows Media Player

Alternatively you can click the **Rip** button on the main menu bar across the top of the screen. By default, all of the tracks are ticked, but you can exclude tracks by clicking to remove the tick.

The Library

After you have copied the CD, its details are displayed in the **Library**, accessed via its own button as shown below. Down the left-hand side of the library is a list of folders similar to the Explorer window in Windows Computer.

Your music is categorized automatically into the **Genre** – **Classical**, **Jazz**, **Rock/Pop**, etc., and you can also select records by **Artist**, **Composer**, **Year Released**, etc. As you can see above, your music is represented graphically – shown by album covers. Sometimes an album picture won't be available; in this case, the Media Player can search the Internet for one. If you have more than one album in a category, they will be displayed as a *stack*; double-click the category to see  the records in that genre. The **Library** allows you to compile your own playlists, with your favourite tracks.

Playing Music from CD or Hard Disc

To play music from a CD, simply insert the CD in the drive
and the media player will start up automatically with the
Now Playing feature selected as described earlier. To play
music which has been copied to your hard disc, start the
media player and open up the **Library**. Select the required
playlist or album from the left-hand panel and click the
Play button to start the music.

Click the **Now Playing** button to display the currently
selected visualization as shown below.

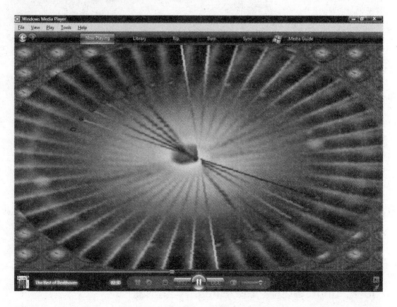

To display all the tracks in the current playlist select **Show
List Pane** off the **Now Playing** drop-down menu.

The Media Guide

Clicking this button connects you to the Internet and the Windows Media Guide. On this page there are  links to various multimedia sources. Here you can select from a range of online music and purchase and download music to be saved on your hard disc. You can also connect to various online radio stations and listen to music directly. You can listen to music and watch videos using a process known as "streaming"; the multimedia files are not recorded on your hard disc but instead you watch them as they are being downloaded. If your Internet connection is via a dial-up modem, the performance of streamed video is very limited. *Broadband connections*, such as ADSL and cable modems, operating many times faster than the traditional modem, are much more suitable for streaming.

Copying or Burning Music to a CD or DVD

Windows Vista includes its own CD/DVD "burning" software, for the copying of data files and multimedia files to disc. Place a blank CD/DVD in the drive. Vista can detect whether you have inserted a CD or DVD.

Now click the **Burn** button and drag the records you want to copy and drop them onto the **Burn List** on the right-hand panel shown below. Now click **Start Burn** to copy the selected music to the CD or DVD.

While the music is being burned to the CD/DVD, the progress of the burn is displayed, as shown on the right. When all of the music has been copied to the CD/DVD, the disc is ejected from the drive.

Watch and Record Digital Television on Your Computer

Introduction

During 2008–2012 the United Kingdom is switching entirely to digital television, in a region-by-region changeover. After the change viewers will typically need either a digital set-top box or a new digital television set, in order to watch any programmes. Various digital services are available; Freeview requires a small initial payment but then makes over 40 TV and radio channels freely available. These include all the present BBC, ITV, Channel 4 and Five channels plus many more. Some existing equipment may not work properly with the new digital services; for example, a VCR may only record the channel you are currently viewing.

However, if you have a modern computer, it already contains most of the equipment needed to watch and record digital television. As one who never got round to fully mastering the intricacies of the humble VCR, I have been amazed at how easily and cheaply you can add excellent quality live digital television viewing and recording to your computer. Perhaps this is not surprising, since digital information is meat and drink to the computer.

The main new component required is a small *TV tuner* as shown below; this simply plugs into a spare USB 2.0 port on your computer. The other end of the tuner has a socket for a normal TV aerial. TV tuners are also available as *expansion cards*, which fit into a slot inside the computer.

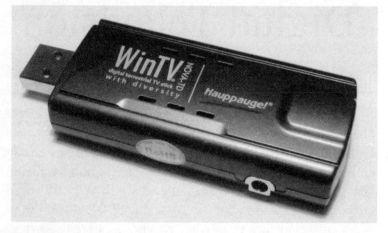

Apart from the tuner itself, there is usually a small aerial, a TV remote control, a software CD and instructions.

Once the computer is set up as a digital television you can:

- Watch live digital television and radio

- Pause, instantly replay then continue live TV programmes

- Use your hard disc to record and replay programmes quickly and easily

- Use a 14-day programme guide to schedule recordings in advance

- Easily delete programmes from the hard disc

- Burn TV programmes to DVD disc in the standard MPEG-2 video format used in DVD players.

The digital television programmes on your computer can be viewed full screen or in a small window, allowing you to carry on with other computing activities at the same time.

A PC television kit will normally include software to control the viewing and recording of television programmes. The Windows Media Center software mentioned on page 8 can also be used to manage the viewing and recording of live television. This software is part of Windows Vista Home Premium, Windows Vista Ultimate and Windows XP Media Center Edition.

Using the Windows Media Center software to set up, watch, record and replay digital television is described later in this chapter.

Where to Set Up a Computer/TV in Your Home

There are various ways in which you might arrange to use a computer to watch television in your home:

The Computer as a Complete Home Media Centre

In this arrangement the TV-equipped computer replaces the traditional TV as a focal point in your lounge or sitting room. This computer can also be used as a music centre and for listening to digital radio. However, dedicating a computer as a media centre in this way may cause problems if one person wants to watch TV and someone else wants to surf the Internet, etc. For this arrangement to work, you really need at least one other computer in the home for the non-TV activities.

An Office Computer with TV Capability

A desktop or laptop computer might be used for normal office functions such as word processing, surfing the Internet, etc., but would also be set up to display and record live television. This computer might be in your home office or in a corner of your living room or bedroom. TV programmes can be viewed directly on the computer monitor and recorded on the hard disc. Programmes can be viewed full screen or in a small window, allowing the computer to be used simultaneously for other tasks.

Television programmes recorded on the computer's hard disc can be played back on the computer monitor or on the main household television via an S-Video cable.

Either a mouse or a remote control can be used to manage the live TV and to schedule recordings, using a 14-day programme guide downloaded from the Internet by the Windows Media Center program. It's very easy to delete old TV programmes to free up hard disc space.

Computer Requirements

A fairly modern computer is needed for this work, with a processor of about 1.7GHz or more. Saved television programmes take up about 1.5GB of hard disc space per hour of television. So you need a hard disc with a lot of free space, perhaps 30GB or more. Even then you will need to keep an eye on the remaining free disc space and regularly delete old TV programmes. If you intend to keep a large library of TV programmes on a hard disc it's worth considering a separate external hard disc which plugs into a USB port. At the time of writing a massive 500GB USB hard drive can be obtained for under £70.

A sound card with speakers is obviously essential and a combined DVD writer drive is needed if you want to burn TV programmes to a DVD (in the MPEG-2 format).

Adding Extra USB 2.0 Ports

The television tuner may require a USB 2.0 port rather than the older and slower USB 1.1 standard. If necessary, you can fit a USB 2.0 PCI expansion card for £20 or less. It's just a case of removing the computer casing and pushing the card into one of the available PCI slots. Spare USB 2.0 ports are useful for connecting many new devices.

To use the Windows Media Center software you need Windows XP Media Center Edition or Windows Vista Home Premium or Windows Vista Ultimate. For maximum performance, Windows Vista requires at least 1GB of main memory or RAM, while 2GB is highly desirable.

PC Television Kits

There are many of these kits available, ranging in price from about £25–£100. The main component is the TV tuner, discussed earlier, which picks up television signals via an aerial and displays them on the computer's monitor. The kit may also include a portable aerial, a TV remote control, a software CD and an instruction manual.

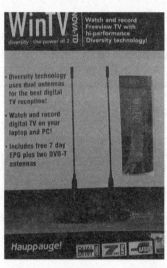

Dual Tuner

A *dual tuner* allows you to watch one digital TV channel while recording another.

Remote Control or Mouse

The kit may include a conventional television remote control, shown on the right. Alternatively the entire process of watching and recording TV programmes can easily be managed using a normal Windows mouse.

Receiving a Signal

It is recommended, at least during the initial setting up process, that the TV tuner is connected to an existing rooftop television aerial which has a strong signal. After detecting the available channels you can then experiment with the small portable aerial provided in the kit.

The tuner can easily be connected to the rooftop aerial using a TV aerial extension lead kit, readily available from any large DIY/electrical store. The kit contains a co-axial extension cable, together with a splitter to divide the original aerial cable into two branches, as shown below. Various co-axial sockets and plugs are also included in the kits and are also sold separately.

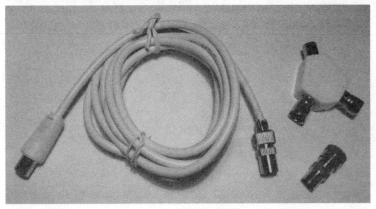

Extension cables are available in various lengths, so, for example, it's quite feasible to run a cable across one or two rooms. Provided the signal from the rooftop aerial is strong, picture quality on the computer should be excellent.

Checking Coverage in Your Area

At the time of writing, the 40 plus Freeview digital channels are available in about 73% of the United Kingdom, increasing to 98.5% after the switchover. It's easy to check the coverage in your own area by connecting to the Web site **www.freeview.co.uk** and entering your post code. An extract from the list of Freeview digital channels available in one particular area is shown below:

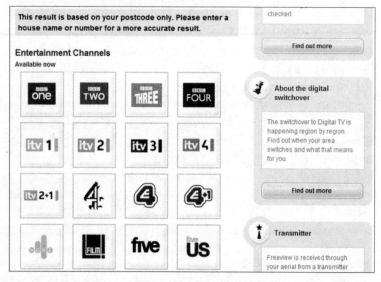

After entering your postcode, the Freeview Web site also tells you when the 2008–2012 region-by-region switchover to digital TV will take place in your area; after that time, traditional analogue televisions without set top boxes will not work. Other relevant Web sites include:

www.digitaltelevision.gov.uk

www.dtg.org.uk/retailer/coverage.html

www.digitaluk.co.uk/postcodechecker

Setting Up the Computer/Television

This section describes the setting up of the television tuner and the detection of the available digital channels. A USB connector at one end of the tuner allows the tuner to be plugged into a spare USB port on the computer; the other end of the tuner has a socket to enable a standard TV aerial cable to be connected to the tuner. As mentioned earlier, this should preferably be a rooftop aerial with a strong signal, at least during the initial setting up.

The Windows operating system should detect the tuner and ask you to insert the CD containing the device drivers. This CD should have been provided in the TV tuner kit. Once the tuner software is installed you can look in the **Device Manager** to see that the tuner is working properly. To open the **Device Manager** click **Start**, **Control Panel** (in **Classic View**) then double-click the icon shown on the right. In this example, a **Hauppauge Nova DVB-T Tuner** is listed under **Sound, video and game controllers**.

Device Manager

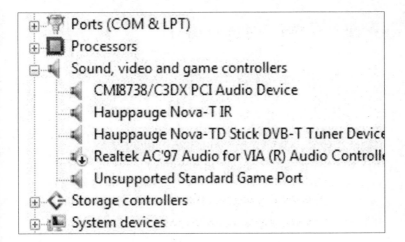

Now double-click the name of the tuner in the **Device Manager**; the **General** tab should open, stating that **This device is working properly**, as shown below.

Windows Vista Compatibility

It's possible that the device driver software on the CD provided with your TV tuner is not compatible with Windows Vista. In this case, if you are using Vista, log on to the Web site of the manufacturer of your TV tuner. Then you should be able to download, free of charge, the latest Vista driver software for your particular TV tuner.

It's usually just a case of downloading the driver file in a compressed format, often as a self-extracting **.EXE** file; then you double-click the name of the downloaded file to extract the compressed file and install the driver software.

Using the Windows Media Center

The first time you launch the Windows Media Center you will need to click the **Start** button, then **All Programs** and **Windows Media Center**. Subsequently you only need to click **Start** and **Windows Media Center**, as shown below.

The first thing you notice is that although the Media Center still has some of the usual window controls, the screen is a striking blue colour and the main menus are quite different.

Using the normal buttons in the top right of the screen to maximize or restore the  window, you can choose to work either full screen or in a small window.

You can move about the screen and select features and options either by using the mouse or using a remote control as used on conventional televisions. The scroll wheel on the mouse is useful for panning the screen vertically; horizontal scrolling is achieved by allowing the cursor to hover over arrows on the screen. Scrolling is achieved using the four arrow buttons on the remote control; the **OK** button is used to make a selection. Select the feature you require, such as **recorded tv**. The selected feature moves to the centre of the screen, from where it is launched.

A **Back** button on the top left-hand corner of the screen allows you to retrace your steps through the various menus. The Windows orb shown on the right can be used to quickly switch the **Media Center** from a small window to full screen.

Along the bottom of the **Media Center** screen there is a complete set of controls equivalent to a television remote control. These include buttons to start recording, change channels, stop a programme, skip forward or back, pause and play/resume a programme and switch between sound and mute.

Detecting the Available Channels

When you first start to use the **Media Center**, there is an option **set up tv**, shown on the right. Or you can select **Tasks**, **settings**, **TV** and **Set Up TV Signal**, as shown below.

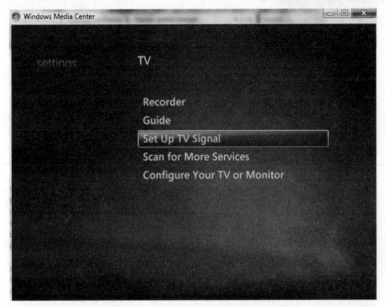

The setup process then follows a wizard-type step-by-step sequence. This is quite simple and only involves clicking **Next** and occasionally providing some local information. For example, you are asked to confirm that your region is the United Kingdom.

(Note in the above menu there is an option to **Configure Your TV or Monitor** to achieve the optimum display. Personally I found no need to adjust the settings on either computer monitor or standard television.)

After entering your postcode you are presented with a list of the available signal providers; these are the television transmitters serving your area. There may be more than one suitable transmitter where you live; for example, in my particular area, the population can tune in to either Waltham on the Wolds in Leicestershire or Sutton Coldfield in the West Midlands.

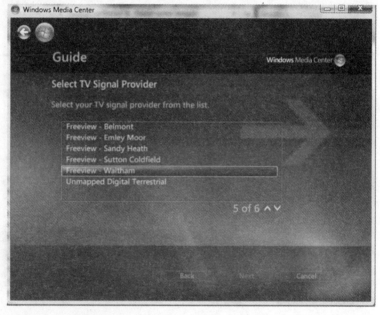

You can check that Freeview is available in your area by logging on to the following Web site:

www.digitaluk.co.uk/postcodechecker

After selecting a transmitter, the Windows Media Center begins the **Scan for Services**, i.e. channels, as shown below.

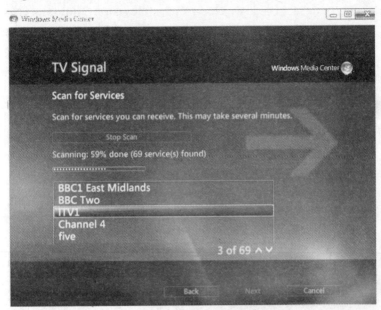

As shown above, 69 channels were found during the above scan, including over 40 television channels and over 25 radio stations. These include the main BBC and ITV channels, etc., plus many others, including Sky news and some channels with less familiar names, as shown below.

The TV Guide

During the setting up process you are given the chance to download a 14-day electronic television **guide**. This includes regional variations determined by your postcode. While your computer is connected to the Internet, the guide is updated automatically, so that it always shows the programmes for the next 14 days.

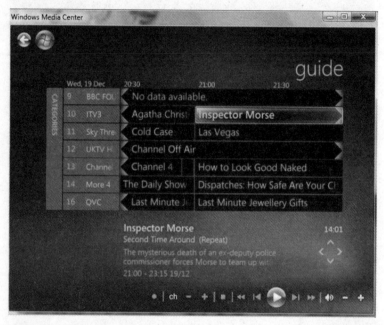

You can scroll around the guide using the four arrows shown above and on the right. Scrolling horizontally displays all of the programmes on a particular channel for the next 14 days. Scrolling vertically displays the programmes for all 69 Freeview and radio channels at a particular time.

If you click on a particular programme in the guide, a screen appears, similar to the one below. This gives a brief summary of the programme and includes a **Record** button for saving an individual programme or **Record Series** to save the remaining episodes in a series.

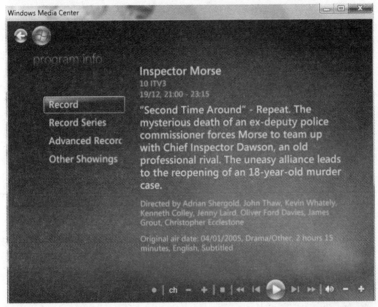

You can return to the guide by clicking the back arrow at the top left-hand corner of the screen. If you click the **Record** button for a programme selected in the guide, a red circle appears in the slot for the programme, as shown below in the **Antiques Roadshow** slot.

Live Television

You can use the back arrows to return to the main screen at any time. Here you can choose one of the main options such as to watch live or recorded television.

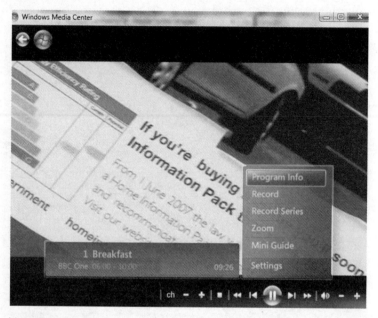

A remote control or a mouse can be used to switch channels or start, stop, pause, or resume a live programme.

Recording Live Television

Right-clicking over the screen while watching live television, brings up the menu shown above on the lower right. This includes options to start (or stop) recording the live TV programme.

Pausing Live Television

While watching live television you can pause and have a good look at a particular screen. Then click **Play** to carry on watching the live programme.

Watching a Recorded Programme

From the main Media Center screen, select **recorded tv**. The list of programmes saved on your hard disc appears, as shown in the example below. As you pass  along the list of recorded programmes, brief details appear underneath the highlighted image.

If you now select the image, further details about the programme appear, together with a menu, as shown on the next page.

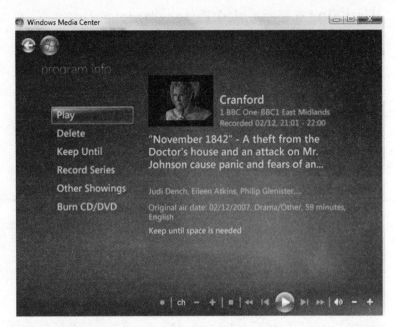

Click **Play** to watch the programme. If the programme has been partially viewed during a previous session, the **Play** button changes to **Resume**.

As shown above, there is a **Delete** button to remove the programme from the hard disc. **Keep Until** presents various options to specify when the recorded programme is to be deleted. **Other Showings** tells you other times when the programme will be broadcast in the current 14-day period.

Burning a TV Programme to DVD

To copy a TV programme using **Burn CD/DVD** above, you must have a DVD writer drive, since video footage usually takes up far too much space for a CD. I have found burning up to 30 minutes of television to a DVD to be satisfactory. Anything much longer can take several hours to copy to DVD, even with a new, quite fast, DVD drive.

TV Programmes Stored as Files on a Hard Disc

One of the advantages of using a computer as a television is the ease with which you can record programmes, play them back and eventually delete them when you've finished. TV programmes are recorded as files on the hard disc, alongside of files for word processing documents, photographs or music, for example.

All of the operations to watch, record and delete TV programmes can be carried out using straightforward, clickable menus and buttons in the Windows Media Center. There is no need to delve into the Windows filing system.

However, if you are sufficiently curious, you can see where the TV programmes are saved as files on your hard disc. Click **Start**, **Computer** or **My Computer** and double-click the hard disc, usually the **C:** drive. In the Windows Explorer, open the folder **Users\Public\Recorded TV** as shown below. Here, for example, you can see that roughly half an hour of "The Nature of Britain" has occupied almost a gigabyte of hard disc space.

Connecting a Computer to a Television Set

My computer/TV sits at one end of the lounge. It's also used as a work machine, especially on winter nights when it's too cold to work outside in the end of the garage that I like to call an office. The layout of the lounge means it's not feasible for everyone to gather round the computer to watch (in any sort of comfort) a two-hour recording of a television classic.

 The answer is simple; a kit costing a few pounds from any of the large electrical stores. The kit contains a long cable known as S-Video and also a sound  cable. Most computers have a round S-Video output on their graphics card as shown on the right above.

The S-Video port shown above connects to an S-Video input on the television. If your television doesn't have an S-Video input, you can buy an adaptor which converts the S-Video cable end connector to a TV SCART connector.

To play the sound through the television, connect a sound cable from the sound card on the computer to the white sound input on the television.

On my system it is necessary to shut down the computer, disconnect the monitor lead from the computer, and connect the S-Video cable to the TV, before restarting the computer. To avoid this, it's possible to obtain graphics cards which support simultaneous output to two monitors or a monitor and a television set.

The quality of the digital TV programmes recorded on the computer is excellent on both the computer monitor and when diverted to the family television.

Key Facts

- *Analogue* television (BBC1, BBC2, ITV, Channel 4 and Five) is currently being phased out.

- By 2012 every region of the country should be converted to *digital* television. Digital television provides clearer pictures with less interference.

- Digital television provides many more channels. Freeview, for example, broadcasts approximately 40 TV channels and 25 radio stations.

- To watch digital television you will need either a new digital television or a set top box. You will probably also want a Personal Video Recorder.

But:

- If you have a modern computer, this already contains most of the equipment needed to watch and record digital television.

- All you need is a *television tuner* costing as little as £25, which simply plugs into the computer.

- It's a good idea to connect the TV tuner to a rooftop TV aerial, using an aerial extension kit.

- The Windows Media Center software is part of popular versions of Windows Vista and XP and contains everything you need to watch and record live television. The Media Center can be operated by either a mouse or television remote control.

- Live television can be *paused* then resumed.

- A cheap S-Video cable enables programmes to be watched on a normal television set.

- Recorded programmes can easily be played and, when no longer needed, deleted from the hard disc.

- An on-going, 14-day *electronic programme guide*, including dates, times and program information can be downloaded from the Internet, allowing you to schedule recordings.

- Programmes can be "burned" to DVD, although copying longer programmes may be very slow.

The Future

The modern computer equipped with a TV tuner, in my experience, provides excellent quality digital television. It is very much cheaper than buying a new digital television set and a Personal Video Recorder. The recording and management of programmes on the computer's hard disc is fast and reliable.

The use of small portable aerials may give a poor signal in some areas. At the time of writing, 73% of the country can receive digital television. This is expected to rise to 98.5% by 2012 after the changeover to digital-only television. Then it's expected that the digital signals will be stronger and portable TV on a laptop will be more viable.

Blue-Ray and HD-DVD

Burning lengthy TV programs onto DVD can be extremely slow with the current technology. This should improve with the new high capacity DVD standards, Blue-Ray and HD-DVD now competing for supremacy. HD (High Definition) television programmes, (though not widely available at the time of writing), will give even better picture and sound quality than the current standard of digital television.

Adding an HD TV tuner to your computer will be a very cost effective and efficient way to participate in this new technology, without having to buy an expensive new HD television and Personal Video Recorder.

Buying and Selling on eBay

Introduction

eBay is the world's leading Internet auction site; you can buy and sell anything under the sun, from the smallest ornament to classic cars, boats, aircraft and houses. Everyone using eBay has to register with their personal details; buyers are able to leave feedback to sellers, commenting on the way the transactions have been handled. The PayPal system insures purchasers' payments against non-delivery of goods; PayPal also ensures instant payment for the seller.

Selling on eBay can be useful to older people in various ways. For example, you might want to:

- Downsize to a smaller home or "declutter" and get rid of a lot of surplus furniture and other chattels.
- You might have a few choice items which you can sell to raise some cash for a special holiday or anniversary celebration, etc.

Registering as a Buyer or Seller

The eBay Web site is launched by entering **www.ebay.co.uk** into a Web browser such as Internet Explorer. To begin using eBay, you first need to register, which is free of charge. Click on the **Register** button near the top of the page, as shown below.

You are presented with a form asking for your personal details such as name, address, phone number and email address. eBay will ask you to create your own **User ID** and **Password**. These will be needed to buy and sell on eBay. Then you must agree to the terms and conditions. Soon after registering eBay sends you an e-mail; this contains a **Confirm Now** button, which you click to complete your eBay registration.

Once you've registered, you have an account with eBay; in future you sign into eBay by entering your **User ID** and **Password** and clicking the **Sign in** button shown on the right.

Buying on eBay

Once signed in, you will see a list of categories of goods available. Almost everything you can think of is listed here – e.g. antiques, books, cars, musical instruments, etc., as shown in the extract on the right.

Shop your Favorite Categories

Antiques
Art
Baby
Books
Business & Industrial
Cameras & Photo
Cars, Boats, Vehicles & Parts
Cell Phones & PDAs
Clothing, Shoes & Accessories
Coins & Paper Money
Collectibles

Click **Visit all categories** to break the entire list into more sub-categories. To display all of the many sub-categories of one main category, just click the category name, such as **Antiques**, for example. This will produce a list of all sorts of antiques such as chairs, clocks, furniture, silver, etc. Also shown is the quantity of those items for sale.

Sometimes the list of goods for sale runs into thousands. For example, at the time of writing, there are 2819 chairs for sale on eBay.

Obviously it would be very time consuming to browse through this entire list; fortunately it's possible to refine your search for the type of chair you are interested in.

For example, if you were looking for a rocking chair, you would type **rocking** in the **Search** bar near the top of the page, as shown below.

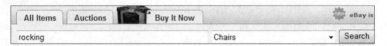

This particular search found 41 rocking chairs. Down the left-hand side of the page, you can also specify exactly what you are looking for, such as the style or age of the chair or the distance you are prepared to travel from your home (based on your postcode). Perhaps you want a Victorian or Edwardian chair, for example. Or you can narrow the search down to chairs in a certain price range.

The Bidding Screen

Part of a typical bidding screen is shown below, listing all items in the auction.

Reading from left to right, the column next to the description shows the number of bids (**6** in the case of the French chair above, for example). Next is shown the price of the item, which changes according to the bidding activity. There is also a **Buy It Now** option, discussed shortly.

Next is the postage cost or other arrangements such as **Pick up only** as shown on the previous page. Chairs, for example, are obviously difficult to post so the buyer might have to collect the item. The words **See description** appear against some items. A more detailed description is displayed by clicking the item name or picture as shown on the previous page. The delivery arrangements and associated costs are included in the description of the item. Perhaps the seller can deliver within, say, a forty mile radius at a particular price. **P** next to the postage column indicates that the seller accepts the PayPal method of payment, as discussed later in this chapter. The far right column gives the time remaining for bids to be submitted in the auction.

Finding Out About the Seller

It's always advisable to find out about the eBay seller before parting with your money. If you click the title of an item on the bidding screen, a more detailed description appears, including a section called **Meet the seller**, which is intended to give you reassurance about their reputation.

Meet the seller

Seller: 24-hour-trading
(847 ⭐) 🏆 **Power Seller**

Feedback: **99.5% Positive**

Member: since 05-Dec-04 in United Kingdom

▪ See detailed feedback
▪ Add to Favourite Sellers
▪ **View seller's other items**

Ask seller a question

✉ Email the seller

The seller's user ID is given to identify them and a figure in brackets gives the number of transactions they've carried out. The coloured star is an 'award' given by eBay for positive feedback.

The extract on the left shows that 99.5% of customers are happy with their transactions with this particular seller.

A lot of the sellers on eBay seem to have a positive rating of around 97-100%. If you wish, you can view the comments made by customers about the service they've received; to do this, click **See detailed feedback**. Here there are also ratings on aspects of service such as delivery time, postage time and communication between buyer and seller. There is also an option **Ask seller a question** to find out more about the item before committing yourself to buying.

The Bidding Process

If an item you're interested in is near the top of the bidding screen, you need to place a bid quickly. Goods being auctioned on eBay are available for a maximum period of ten days, after which bidding is closed. New items are added to the bottom of the list and, as time goes by, they move upwards. As they move up, the time remaining to bid is counting down and is displayed next to the item, as shown below.

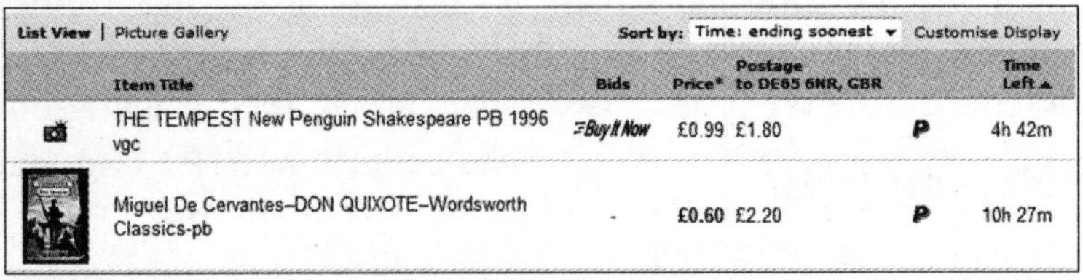

List View	Picture Gallery		Sort by: Time: ending soonest ▾		Customise Display	
	Item Title	Bids	Price*	Postage to DE65 6NR, GBR		Time Left ▴
📷	THE TEMPEST New Penguin Shakespeare PB 1996 vgc	=Buy It Now	£0.99	£1.80	ℙ	4h 42m
🖼	Miguel De Cervantes–DON QUIXOTE–Wordsworth Classics-pb	-	£0.60	£2.20	ℙ	10h 27m

When there is less than an hour to go, the time remaining is highlighted in red. You may want to place a bid early, say, when there are eight days left. However, this gives other bidders plenty of time to outbid you. A tactical move would be to bid near the end of the auction, when you are more likely to win the item at a price you want to pay.

To bid for something, simply click on its title and you will be taken to a screen showing more details of the item and bidding information, as shown below.

If there are no bids, then there will be a **Starting bid** figure, which has been set by the seller as the minimum price. You may enter a bid equal to this or higher in the **Your maximum bid** box. Click on **Place Bid** to confirm your choice.

If other people have already placed bids, then there will be a **Current bid** figure instead of the **Starting bid** figure. When you are competing with other bidders, eBay automatically places bids for you (up to your maximum bid, if necessary) – you don't have to keep putting in bids yourself.

Competing Bids

Suppose two people, Smith and Jones want to bid for the same item. Smith might decide that the maximum price they're willing to pay is, for example, £50. Jones enters their maximum price of, say, £30. eBay will then place a bid which slightly exceeds Jones' maximum, for example £30.10. This is the new current price of the item. eBay will notify Jones that their maximum bid is lower (they have been outbid).

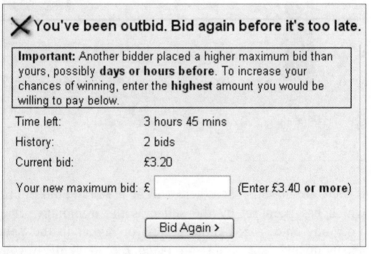

Jones may then raise their maximum price, say to £35. This pushes the current price up to £35.10, which is still well within the maximum price of Smith, so they are still winning. eBay will keep bidding on behalf of Smith until it just exceeds Jones' maximum price. If bidding activity stops before it reaches Smith's maximum price, then Smith will only have to pay that lesser amount.

The Reserve Price

Some sellers set a **Reserve price** – the minimum price they will accept for the item. The reserve price is higher than the starting price given and is not made known to the buyer. It may seem a little strange to have a starting price which falls below what the seller is willing to accept, but this is just a tactic to attract bidders. If the bidding price does not reach the reserve there will be no sale and the bidding screen will display the message **Reserve not met**. This is illustrated on the extract below; there are only sixteen minutes fifty-nine seconds left before the end of the auction, so it's quite possible this item will not sell.

Current bid:	**£510.00**
	Reserve not met
Your maximum bid: £ [ ]	**Place Bid >**
	(Enter £520.00 or more)
End time:	**16 mins 59 secs**
	(05-Nov-07 14:55:19 GMT)

Buy It Now and Best Offer

Although eBay is an auction site, it's also possible to buy goods without bidding and competing with other buyers. The **Buy It Now** option allows you to buy an item at a stated price, as shown below. It's likely that the seller wants a quick sale, rather than waiting for bids to come in.

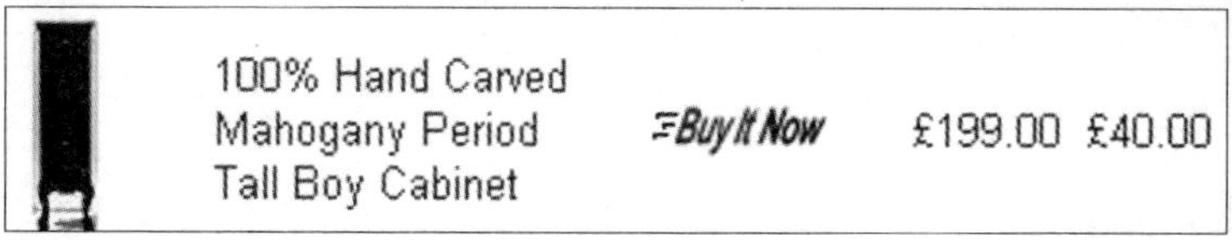

	100% Hand Carved Mahogany Period Tall Boy Cabinet	＝Buy It Now	£199.00 £40.00

Sometimes it is possible to negotiate a price. This can only be done when you see **Buy It Now or Best Offer** as shown below. You simply put in an offer for the item (there is no minimum amount you can offer) which becomes binding if accepted by the seller.

Some sellers actually combine bidding with the chance to **Buy It Now**. The **Buy It Now** price is higher than the **Starting bid**. The buyer can place a bid lower than the **Buy It Now** price and hope they win at the cheaper price. Or if they're really keen to get the item, they can use the **Buy It Now** option, without worrying about being outbid.

Starting bid   **£14.90**

Your maximum bid: **£** [   ]   **Place Bid >**

(Enter £14.90 or more)

Buy It Now price: **£17.90**   **Buy It Now >**

Watching an Item in an Auction

On the bidding screen, simply click **Watch this item** and the following message will appear.

You are watching this item in <u>My eBay</u> (1 item)

You then need to open **My eBay** by clicking the button near the top right of the screen, as shown below.

The item you are watching will appear in **My eBay** as shown below.

Items I'm Watching (1 item)   <u>Customise Displa</u>

Show: **All** | <u>Active</u> (1) | Ended (0)

		Current Price	Postage Cost	Bids	Seller ID	Bid Assistant Group	Time Left ⌃	Acti
☐	📷	NORTH WALES GHOSTS - RICHARD FELIX						
☐		£4.99	£1.49	0	localhistoryandghostdvds (117 ⭐)	--	11m	

This enables you to keep an eye on the bidding activity without committing yourself to bidding or buying. You can always delete this entry if you wish.

My eBay

The **My eBay** screen is basically a summary of all your current and recent activities on eBay. It shows items you are bidding for, items you are selling, items won and items lost and generally keeping track of all your transactions. Also included are useful reminders of any auctions that are ending soon. It's a very helpful screen to anyone using eBay regularly.

Paying for an Item

Once you've won an item on eBay, you will be notified by e-mail, with an instruction to pay. Click the yellow **Pay Now** box and then select your chosen payment method on the seller's invoice. There are several different ways of paying although not all of them are accepted by some sellers.

PayPal

You can pay by PayPal, postal order/bankers draft, or personal cheque. PayPal is the method preferred by eBay and is regarded as the safest. There is a PayPal Protection Program which guarantees protection up to a certain limit and includes cover if your goods are unsatisfactory and protects your bank details against fraud. You need to sign up for a PayPal account, which is free to buyers. To do this click **Buy** at the top of the screen.

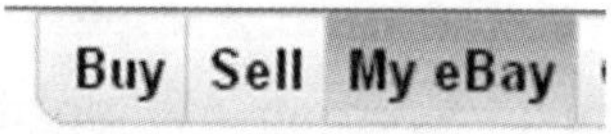

This takes you to the **Buy** page, on the right of which is a section called **Buying Resources** shown below

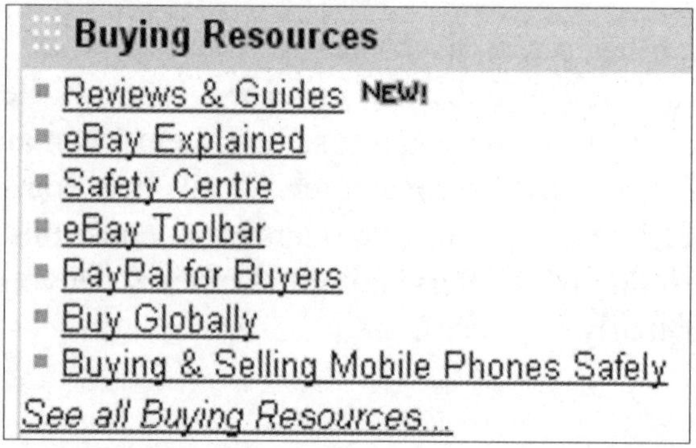

From the above list, select **PayPal for Buyers**.

This takes you to a page giving an overview of eBay.

What is PayPal?

PayPal is the safe, easy way to pay online. It enables you to send and receive money online without sharing your financial details.

Major features of PayPal include:

- Your financial details are not given to the seller
- It's free and payment is instant
- Your payment is protected up to a value of £500 – safeguarding you against non-delivery.

Click on **Sign up now** and a **Create Your PayPal** account screen appears. Then enter your e-mail address and choose and confirm a password for your PayPal account. After reading the **User Agreement** click on **Agree and Sign Up**. eBay will ask you for some bank details and your PayPal account should be ready to use..

Cheque or Postal Order

Should you decide to pay by other means, say a cheque or postal order, you would mark this on the invoice sent to you by the seller. The seller's address should be included on the invoice; if not you have to contact the seller by e-mail and ask for the address. (You can e-mail the seller from the bidding screen).

Once you have sent your payment, you then go to **My eBay**. The item you have bought will appear here and it's helpful if you mark it **Payment Sent** by selecting this from the drop-down menu.

The pound sign icon shown below changes to blue to confirm payment sent. Notice how the menu now reads **Unmark as Payment Sent**.

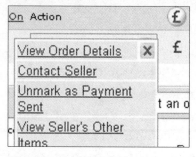

You could also choose **Contact Seller** from this menu and type a short message, letting them know that you have sent your payment to them. This is courteous and may help you to receive positive feedback from the seller.

Leaving Feedback

Once you've received your item, you can leave feedback on how satisfactory (or otherwise) the transaction was. For instance, is the item in the condition as described by the seller? How quick was the delivery? Was it well-packaged? These are all considerations to take into account when leaving feedback. On the drop-down menu shown above (headed **View Order Details**), there is an option to **Leave Feedback**. You will be asked to rate the transaction overall

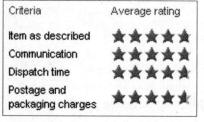

as being positive, neutral or negative and to leave a short comment, justifying why you found it positive or otherwise.

Next you can rate the transaction in its various parts, such as communication between buyer and seller, dispatch time, etc., as can be seen above left.

Once feedback has been confirmed, you cannot change it. Feedback is valued by both customer and seller and obviously affects their reputation, so it's worth giving it some time and careful thought. If you then return to **My eBay** and look at your transaction, you will see that the feedback icon (represented by a star), as shown on the right, has changed to blue.

When the seller has left some positive feedback, the circle with a cross will also turn blue. To read what they've said about you, click **Feedback** under **My Account** in the left-hand column on **My eBay**.

Feedback as a seller	**Feedback as a buyer**	All Feedback	Feedback left for others

Ratings mutually withdrawn: 0   Bid retractions (last 12 months): 0

24 Feedback received

Feedback / Item	From Seller
➕ Prompt payer., good ebayer, thank you	lilleypad07 (3359 ⭐)
Murder Crime and Punishement in Derby Richard Felix (#270192606311)	--
➕ excellent fast payment	grisslaw3 (683 ⭐)
Duran Duran - Red Carpet Massacre (2007) (#180182197900)	--
➕ A pleasure to deal with. Recommended.	4848alexander (676 ⭐)
THE RIVER TWEED - JOHN RICHARD THACKRAH - HB - 1980 (#190159808061)	--
➕ great ebayer very fast payment, great communication, thankyou	felixfilmsltd (178 ⭐)
NEW GHOSTS OF ANNESLEY HALL-RICHARD FELIX-MOST HAUNTED	--

Feedback from Sellers

In early 2008, eBay decided that, from May 2008, sellers would not be able to leave negative or neutral feedback about buyers, as these communications were thought to be causing problems and slowing down trade. Buyers can leave positive, neutral and negative feedback about sellers.

Selling on eBay

If you've a lot of unwanted items that are cluttering up your home, then it makes sense to turn them into cash. With eBay, you can sell just about anything you want. Even cars, boats and aeroplanes can be traded, as well as smaller items such as jewellery and ornaments.

Once you've have decided what to sell, then it's a good idea to look at similar items on eBay. This should give you an idea of the value and the way they're described.

Including a Photograph

A good photograph is bound to help to sell your item. A digital camera is recommended because it's very easy to transfer the photos onto a folder on the computer. From this folder, the photo can then be uploaded on to the eBay Web site. (Traditional photos made on film need to input into the computer using a digital scanner).

Experiment with lighting and various backgrounds to the object – a poor photo is likely to put customers off and will not do justice to the item you're selling. When you've taken the photograph, it must be transferred to the computer and saved on the hard disc as a file.

Using a special cable normally provided with a digital camera, connect the camera to one of the USB ports on the front or back of the computer.

A small menu then appears on the screen, asking you what you would like to do with the picture.

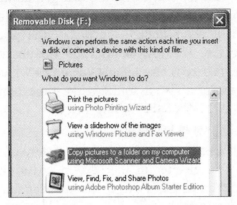

Select **Copy pictures to a folder...** as shown above. The Windows **Scanner and Camera Wizard** is launched and leads you step-by-step through some simple instructions to save your pictures onto the hard disc. Your photo(s) appear on the screen and you simply tick the check boxes next to the pictures to be copied.

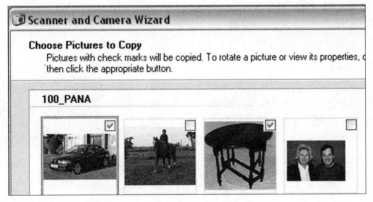

You are then asked for a name for the photos and to browse for a folder location to save them in.

Fees for Selling on eBay

When you sell on eBay, you are charged an **Insertion Fee**. This fee varies according to the **Starting** or **Reserve Price** you place on your item – the higher the price, then the higher the fee. The lowest insertion fee charged is just a few pence. There is also a **Final Value Fee** which is charged once the item has been sold. At the time of writing, this represents 5.25% of the selling price. If there is no sale, then no **Final Value Fee** is charged.

To sell on eBay, you need to be registered, as described earlier in this chapter in the section covering buying on eBay. It is then necessary to **Create a seller's account**, after clicking on **Sell** at the top of the page. This involves giving your bank details, such as bank address, sort code, account number, etc. These are safeguarded by eBay's protection policy.

Completing the Selling Form

It is then a case of filling in a few details about your item.

Sell
ⓘ Sign in to see your saved information.
List your item for sale
Enter 3-5 words about your item. For example: New Toy Story DVD
[   ]
◉ Quick Sell (not suitable for vehicles)
List your item quickly using the most popular options
○ Advanced Sell (Sell Your Item Form)
Access to all the options (reserve price, subtitle, scheduled listing and more)
Start selling

eBay asks you to describe it in 3–5 words and then you select either **Quick Sell** or **Advanced Sell**. **Quick Sell** is good enough for most items. Next click **Start selling**.

You are then taken to a **Create Your Listing** screen where you enter the full title of your item in the bar under **Create a descriptive title for your item**. Next choose the relevant category for your item, e.g. **Music>CDs**.

Then under **Bring your item to life with pictures**, click **Add a photo** as shown below.

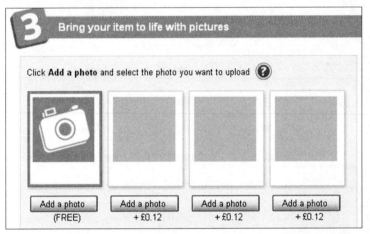

Click on **Add a photo** and a window appears where you can click **Browse...** to find the folder where your picture is stored. Then click **Upload** and in a few seconds the picture is transferred to eBay. The first photo is free but if you wish to add more there is a small charge, as shown above. To attract more buyers you can have your picture displayed in the list of items resulting from a search (at a cost of five pence); to do this, tick the check box next to **Gallery Picture** as shown below.

☑ Gallery Picture: Include a small picture of your item in search results to attract more buyers.
(£0.05) (recommended) ❷

Next you are asked to **Describe the item you're selling** and this is your chance to include as much information as possible. You are provided with quite a generous window in which to enter the description, rather like a simple word processor, as shown below.

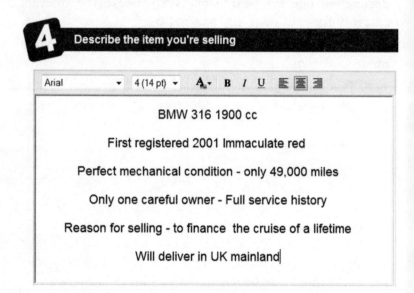

It's important that you are totally honest about any faults in the item and your reasons for selling. Any dishonesty will cause disappointment to the buyer and you might suffer financial loss and possible legal action; problems with the transaction will result in negative feedback against you as a seller. This would make it very difficult for you to continue to sell things on eBay in the future.

Setting the Starting Price

After the description, you then choose a starting price for your auction as shown below, next to **Start auction bidding**.

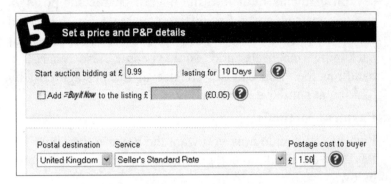

This may take a little consideration. If the price is too high, it will not attract bidders. It's likely there will be plenty of other items identical to yours being auctioned, so your starting price needs to be competitive. A low price would be more attractive to potential bidders, but you can never be sure how much interest will be generated. You may only get one bidder for your item. Therefore if you start low, this could well be the price your item eventually sells for.

Duration of the Auction

You can also choose the duration of the auction in days – the choices are 3, 5, 7 and 10. If you wish to give customers the chance to purchase your item instantly, rather than bidding, then select **Buy It Now**. The fee for this is five pence.

Charging for Postage

The cost of postage and packing to the customer is charged separately from the bidding/buy it now price. There are several elements built into the overall charge for postage. Actual postage costs for different parcels can be found from the Post Office. Then you have your cost of packaging materials and some people also charge a handling fee. You can get an idea of the postage cost by looking at similar items on eBay.

Payment Methods

Finally you decide how you want the buyer to pay you. For PayPal you need to enter your email address as shown below.

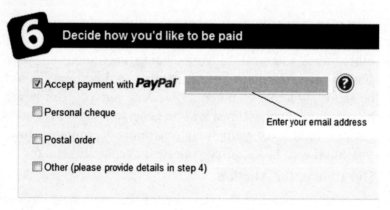

eBay states that PayPal is the easiest and safest option for buyers; as a seller you don't have to wait for cheques to arrive and then be cleared.

You can then **Save and review** your listing and have the opportunity to amend any details you are not happy with. Once you are satisfied, click **Place listing** and your item will be placed on eBay and the auction begins.

Questions from Potential Buyers

During the time your goods are on sale, you may have potential buyers asking questions about them.

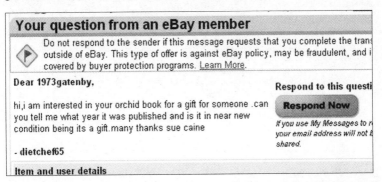

These questions show an interest in what you are selling so it's a good idea to respond quickly before they lose interest. Obviously it's advisable to answer questions honestly and to be courteous with the potential customer.

Completing the Sale

All being well you will be notified by eBay of the good news, as shown below.

As the above extract shows, you need to click **Send Invoice** to begin the sale transaction.

An invoice then appears, giving you the option to update the payment information – you might want to include a discount, for example.

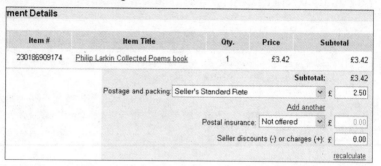

Another section on the invoice is **Enter Payment Instructions & Personal Message**. Some things would require special instructions, for example to arrange the collection or delivery of an item which was too big to post, such as a bike, for example.

You can also use this opportunity to send a friendly message to your customer.

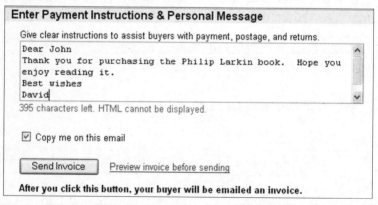

Once the invoice is complete, click **Send Invoice** and the buyer will receive it and an instruction to pay you.

Setting up a PayPal Account

PayPal is the most popular payment method and you will be e-mailed once this has been made. If you're new to eBay it's a good idea to set up a PayPal account straightaway.

Simply click on **Sell** at the top of the screen and in the bottom left you will see **Selling safely**.

Selling safely
How to sell safely
PayPal Seller Protection
Manage bidders

More help?
Selling Forums
Get tips from others
eBay Help
Need to report a problem?

Now select **PayPal Seller Protection**; The **PayPal Auction Tools** screen appears and you need to click **Sign Up** at the top, which will take you to the screen below.

Sign Up for a PayPal Account

PayPal. Safe. Simple. Smart.
Find out more about PayPal.

◉ **Personal Account**
   Ideal for shopping online. Pay without revealing your debit or credit card numbers, your bank account details, or entering your address details for every transaction. Remember, it's free to send funds to family and friends.

◯ **Premier Account**
   Perfect for buying and selling on eBay or merchant websites. Accept all payment types for low fees. Do business under your own name.

◯ **Business Account**
   The right choice for your online business. Accept all payment types for low fees. Do business under a company or group name. Learn more

---

As can be seen above, the type of account needs to be chosen. For buying and selling under your own name, the **Premium Account** is probably the most appropriate. Click **Continue** at the bottom and a form appears, asking for details such as name, address, country of citizenship, telephone number, e-mail address and a password.

Then you have to read the terms and conditions and agree to them. There is also a security check to prevent computer systems signing up for an account. Click **Sign Up**.

After confirming your e-mail address, you will be sent an e-mail giving you a confirmation number. Next return to eBay and enter the confirmation number.

It is then necessary to provide details of your bank account, including bank name and address, account number, sort code and name of account holder.

Dispatching An Item

As PayPal provides instant payment, you need to dispatch your item as soon as possible. Obviously if the customer decides to pay by cheque, then it would be wise to wait until the cheque has cleared before posting.

Small, fragile items to be posted should be carefully protected using packing such as bubble wrap, newspapers, polystyrene or padded envelopes.

You may wish to include a dispatch note of your own design or an acknowledgement thanking the customer for their purchase. It's a good idea to send the item by recorded delivery; this costs a little extra, but the parcel will be signed for at its destination. After posting an item, an e-mail to the buyer telling them their purchase is on its way will usually be appreciated. Go to **My eBay** and in the section called **Items I've Sold** go to the transaction and in the little drop-down menu, click on **Mark as Dispatched**. The white dispatched cube icon shown below then changes to blue.

The drop-down menu just mentioned is very helpful during your transactions. As can be seen to the left, there are a number of different things that can be done. The **Contact Buyer** is probably the most useful because regular communication is a key aspect of trading on eBay.

Leaving Feedback

At the end of a transaction, it's possible to leave feedback on how it all went. Simply click **Leave Feedback** at the top as shown on the above menu.

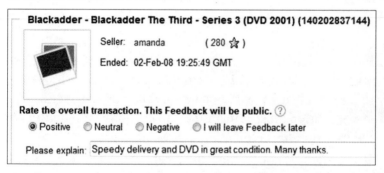

The buyer can select a radio button, as shown above, to rate the transaction positive, neutral or negative and add a few words of further explanation. The seller is only able to leave positive feedback about a buyer. It's important for the buyer to leave accurate feedback; this may act as either a reassurance or a warning to potential customers in the future. Similarly, leaving unjustified negative feedback could damage the reputation of a genuine and honest seller.

When Your Item Does Not Sell

You may well be wondering what happens if, at the end of the auction, you do not manage to sell your goods. If you wish, you can relist the items. There are several ways to do this but the easiest is probably by responding to an e-mail from eBay. This is sent automatically when there is no sale.

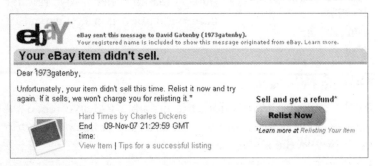

Simply click on **Relist Now** as shown in the above e-mail. An insertion fee is still payable, but eBay offers an insertion fee credit if the item sells this time around. So your insertion fee will be refunded. Any further relistings of the same item will not be eligible for the credit. The starting price must remain the same in order to qualify for the insertion fee credit.

If the item is not selling, then perhaps there is too much competition on eBay – if there are lots of similar items to yours and hardly any demand, then the time is not right to sell. Perhaps you need to consider marketing factors such as price and presentation, taking more care with any photographs and descriptions.

Joining the eBay community is very enjoyable and a good way to learn about buying and selling; What better way to clear out your attic or garage and raise some useful cash – with all the excitement of the live auction?

Getting the Best from Your Computer

Introduction

Modern computers are very reliable if treated sensibly; for a good many years I have had three or more computers up and running at home and there have been no major problems. These are not top of the range, expensive machines but budget computers, including one I assembled myself. (It's not that difficult – it's mainly just a case of plugging the components together. The hardest part is diagnosing faults when things do go wrong).

The biggest threat might occur if you let children or grandchildren "improve" your computer by changing a few settings or installing some new software. As a former teacher I know that some children have the ability to wreak havoc, either accidentally or even deliberately, when let loose on a computer. If you're using a computer for serious work, whether business, social or charitable, it's a good idea if that machine is kept separate from any computer used by other people for entertainment.

This chapter describes some simple steps you can take to keep your computer running at its best level of performance; they don't require any special skill, won't cost a lot of money and most will only take a few minutes.

Spring-clean Your Hard Disc

During normal running, your computer creates a lot of temporary files on the hard disc. When you browse the Internet, the content of Web pages is saved so the site can be viewed more quickly at a later time. When using a program like Word 2007, a lot of temporary files are created. These take up disc space and if ignored for a long time may cause the computer to run slowly.

To remove these redundant files cluttering up your hard disc, run **Disk Cleanup**, once a week say, by selecting **Start**, **All Programs**, **Accessories**, **System Tools** and **Disk Cleanup**.

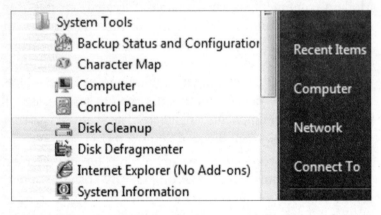

After you've used **Disk Cleanup** once, in future the program can be launched straightway from the main **Start** menu. A window opens giving you the chance to clean up just your own files or the files of all users of the computer. After making a selection, you choose the drive you wish to clean up – usually drive **(C:)**. **Disk Cleanup** then takes a few minutes to calculate how much disc space can be saved by deleting unnecessary files.

After calculating the potential gain in recovered disc space, the unnecessary files are listed, as shown below.

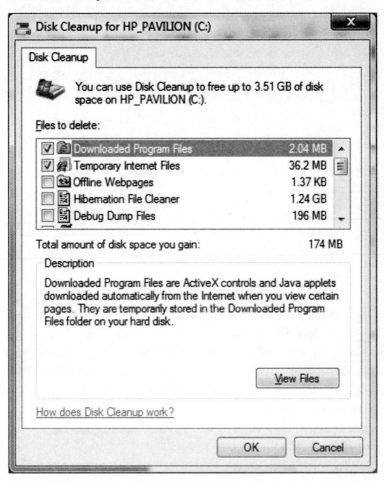

When you click on an entry, such as **Temporary Internet Files**, the purpose of the files is explained in the **Description** panel as well as guidance on the effects of removing them.

Decide which files to delete and mark their check boxes with a tick. The amount of free disc space to be gained is displayed in the window shown on the previous page. When you've marked which files are to be deleted, click **OK** and the window shown below appears.

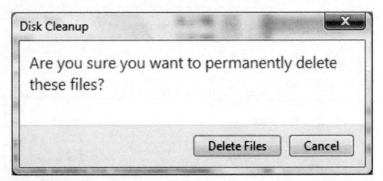

Click the **Delete Files** button shown above to complete the cleanup operation.

You can quickly check the free space on your hard disc by clicking the **Start** orb,

then click **Computer** off the **Start** menu. The extract from the **Computer** window below shows that the hard disc drive **(C:)** initially had **24.0GB** free space. After running **Disk Cleanup**, the amount of free space increased to **24.2GB**. Much greater

savings of several gigabytes can be made using **Disk Cleanup**. For example, you might delete the **Hibernation File**, shown on the previous page, if you don't use the hibernation power setting on your computer. Also by deleting **Temporary files** stored in a **TEMP** folder and not modified in the last week.

Using Disk Defragmenter

After you've been using your computer for a while, many files will have been repeatedly modified and resaved. The original files and the changes may become separated, scattered about the hard disc in different places. This will impair the performance of the computer when it tries to open a file which is spread around many different locations; *defragmentation* is a process which rearranges the hard disc to make it run more efficiently. In Windows Vista, the **Disk Defragmenter** program is scheduled to run automatically. Alternatively it can be launched by clicking the **Start** orb then selecting **All Programs**, **Accessories**, **System Tools** and **Disk Defragmenter**.

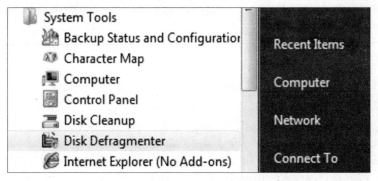

After you've used **Disk Defragmenter** the first time, the program can be launched in future by clicking its name, which by now will be listed on the **Start** menu.

The **Disk Defragmenter** window opens, as shown on the next page. In this particular example, the **Disk Defragmenter** program has been scheduled to run once a week, but you can change this if you wish after clicking **Modify schedule**....

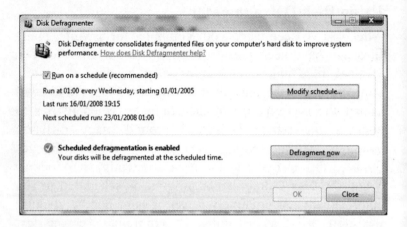

Please also note in the **Disk Defragmenter** window above, the **Defragment now** button allows you to manually start an immediate defragmentation whenever you think it might be beneficial. Select the drive you wish to defragment, usually **(C:)** then click the **Defragment** button.

The defragmentation process may take several minutes or a few hours, depending on the size and state of the hard disc. Fortunately you can continue to use the computer while the **Disk Defragmenter** program is running.

Good Housekeeping

It's recommended that, in order to keep your computer running efficiently, **Disk Cleanup** and **Disk Defragmenter** are run regularly – at least once a week, especially if the computer is heavily used. If the computer appears to be running slowly for no obvious reason, it may be worth carrying out a manual defragmentation.

Speed Up Your Computer with ReadyBoost

ReadyBoost is a feature of Windows Vista which enables certain removable storage devices to increase the speed of the computer; the storage capacity of the removable device is used to supplement the memory (RAM) of the computer. Some USB flash drives, also known as data "dongles" and mass storage devices, can be used for this purpose.

Flash drives are very easy to install; they simply plug into one of the small rectangular USB ports on the computer

– you don't even need to switch your machine off.

Not all flash drives are compatible with ReadyBoost – you need to buy a flash drive displaying a small sticker with the words **Enhanced for Windows ReadyBoost**. A suitable drive is the SanDisk Cruzer Micro USB Flash Drive 4.0GB, which can be bought for well under £15.

The USB ports should be of the latest USB 2.0 standard – not the slower USB 1.0 type used on earlier machines. If necessary, an older machine having only USB 1.0 ports can be upgraded easily and cheaply by fitting an expansion card with several USB 2.0 ports, as described later in this book. This modification will also be very useful if you want to add other devices which may benefit from extra USB 2.0 ports, such as a printer, USB modem, digital camera or TV tuner, for example.

When the USB flash drive is plugged into a USB 2.0 port, it is detected and, in this example, designated **Removable Disk (F:)**. Windows automatically installs the necessary software for the flash drive. The **AutoPlay** window then opens including an option to speed up the system using **Windows ReadyBoost**.

If your flash drive is not suitable to be used with ReadyBoost, the **Properties** dialogue box displays the statement shown below, starting **This device does not....**.

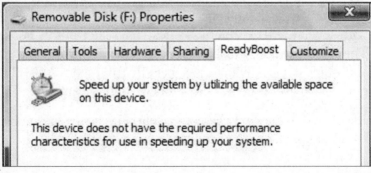

If your flash drive does have the required performance, i.e. enough *fast flash memory* as it is known, the **ReadyBoost** tab in the **Properties** dialogue box opens, as shown below. This allows you to allocate some of the space on the flash drive to be used by ReadyBoost to speed up the system. Windows recommends the amount of flash drive space to use – normally about one to three times the amount of RAM installed in the computer. Move the slider shown below, next to **3770MB**, to set the reserved space yourself.

ReadyBoost is a quick and easy way to supplement the computer's memory or RAM. However, it's often very beneficial to install extra memory modules or RAM; as discussed in the next chapter "Useful Hardware Additions", it's a simple task which anyone can accomplish.

The Windows Security Center

You can carry out a check of all the security
features in Windows Vista by launching the
Windows Security Center. Click **Start**, **Control
Panel** and double-click the **Security Center**
icon as shown on the right. You are

Security
Center

recommended to make sure that the main security features
are either switched **On** or marked **OK** as shown below.

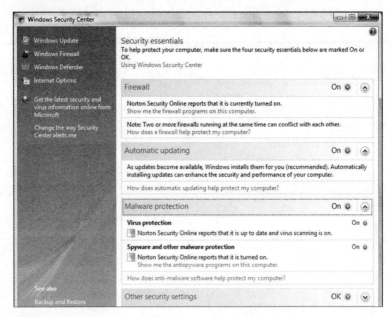

In the **Windows Security Center** shown above, each of the
main features, **Firewall**, **Automatic updating** and **Malware
protection**, etc., has been expanded to give more
information. This is done by clicking
the downward pointing arrowhead, as
shown here on the right. In the **Security
Centre** as shown above, click the upward pointing
arrowhead to collapse each security feature.

The Windows Firewall

The firewall is a piece of software or hardware designed to protect your computer from criminal activity such as hackers or fraudsters. Windows has its own firewall which should be turned on, unless you have installed an Internet security package such as Norton, F-Secure or McAfee.

Turning Windows Firewall On

Select **Start**, **Control Panel**, then double-click **Windows Firewall** and click **Change settings**. If necessary click the circular radio button to make sure Windows Firewall is **On**.

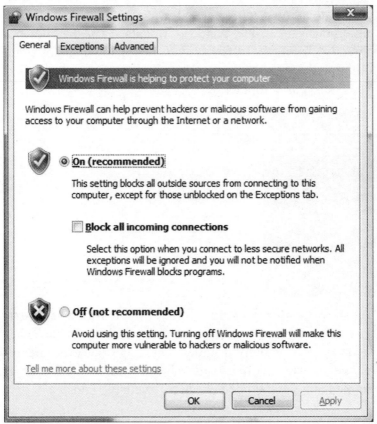

Automatic Updating

Windows Update provides regular modifications to the Windows operating system; these are often designed to make the system more secure and take the form of a small piece of software or "patch". Windows Update allows you to schedule your computer to check for the latest updates and download them to your computer from the Internet. Sometimes completely new versions of a major Windows component such as the Windows Media Player may be available as an update.

Windows Update can be launched initially from the **Start** menu, then **All Programs** and **Widows Update**. The next time you want to use **Windows Update** it can be launched directly from the **Start** menu. As shown below, the Windows Update screen opens and displays the update status of your computer.

As shown above, you are informed when **Windows Update** last checked for available updates and the date when updates were actually installed. Clicking **Check for updates** above on the left-hand side allows you to carry out an immediate, unscheduled check for available updates.

Change settings, shown on the left of the image on the previous page, enables you to schedule automatic daily or weekly checks for updates.

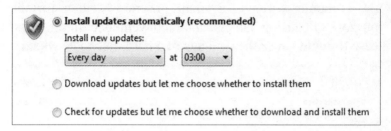

The radio buttons (circles) above allow you to choose whether you want automatic installation of updates or to control the downloading and installation yourself.

Clicking **View update history** shown on the left of the image on the previous page shows the updates that have been installed on one particular computer. The list can be scrolled to view almost an entire year of updates.

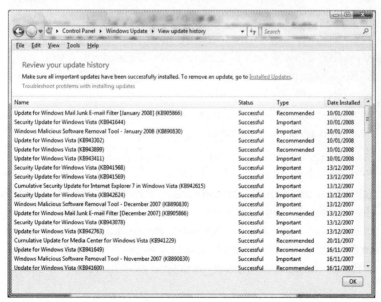

Malware Protection

Malware is an abbreviation for malicious software and refers to computer viruses and other malevolent programs; the computer virus is a small program written for the purpose of causing damage and inconvenience. In the worst case it might cause the contents of a hard disc to be wiped.

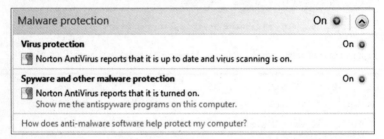

The **Malware protection** extract from the **Windows Security Center** shown above reports on any anti-virus software installed on your computer. It's essential that you have an anti-virus program installed and that this is regularly updated so that it can detect and deal with the latest viruses.

Well known anti-virus software includes Norton AntiVirus, McAfee VirusScan, F-Secure Anti-Virus and AVG Anti-Virus. Many companies also produce complete Internet security packages which include anti-virus software as well as firewalls and protection against *spyware* – software designed to collect personal information from a computer.

Anti-virus/Internet Security packages typically costs £20–£40 and this includes the software CD/DVD and a year's updates of virus definitions. Updates are normally downloaded automatically from the Internet. Many companies now allow one software package to be legally installed on up to three computers. Subscriptions to an anti-virus package are normally renewed annually.

12

Useful Hardware Additions

Introduction

The old adage "if it ain't broke don't fix it" is just as relevant to computers as it is to cars or any other devices which people, predominantly men, like to tinker with. However, there are some simple hardware additions which anyone can usefully make to a computer; they are inexpensive, don't require any skill or technical knowledge and yet can bring major benefits. The hardware modifications discussed in this chapter are:

- Adding extra memory or RAM
- Fitting a USB 2.0 PCI expansion card
- Installing a wireless router and wireless network
- Using a Flat Screen TFT Monitor
- Changing to a wireless keyboard and mouse.

Sensitive components inside of a computer, such as memory modules or expansion cards, can be damaged by static electricity from your body. Therefore before doing any hardware modifications to a computer:

- Switch off and unplug the computer
- Get rid of your static electricity by touching a grounded metal object such as a water pipe; alternatively wear a special anti-static wrist strap.

The Memory or RAM

The memory is crucial to the efficient running of your computer; if you don't have enough memory programs will run very slowly or perhaps not at all. The memory (also known as RAM or Random Access Memory) is a set of chips, as shown below, which acts as a store for the data or information typed in at the keyboard or loaded from disc.

The memory also holds the programs that you're currently using. The memory is said to be volatile – when the computer is switched off the contents of the memory are lost. Modern programs, especially in Windows Vista and Office 2007, with all of their graphics, windows and icons, demand massive amounts of memory. Photographs and video are also very hungry for memory.

Until recently it was common for computers to be sold with 512MB or 1024MB (i.e. 1GB) of memory. Now, especially with the arrival of Windows Vista, 1GB is regarded as the bare minimum and 2GB is becoming normal.

Adding memory is one of the easiest ways of improving the performance of a computer – it's only a 10 minute job.

Jargon

1MB (megabyte) is the amount of memory needed to store approximately 1 million characters (letters, numbers, punctuation marks, etc.)

1GB (gigabyte) is 1024MB.

Adding Extra Memory (RAM)

To find out how much memory (RAM) your computer has, in Windows Vista select **Start**, **Computer** and **System properties**, as shown in the example below. In Windows XP select **Start**, **My Computer** and **View system information**.

System	
Rating:	2.7 Windows Experience Index : Unrated
Processor:	Intel(R) Celeron(R) CPU 2.80GHz 2.80 GHz
Memory (RAM):	1279 MB
System type:	32-bit Operating System

Increasing the memory involves taking the cover off the computer and plugging in extra memory modules into slots in the motherboard.

Or you might replace say, a 512MB module with a *compatible* 1GB or 2GB module. Release the clips at the ends of the module then gently pull the module away from the slot in the motherboard. Always hold the memory modules by the edges and never touch the chips themselves or the connecting pins. If buying from the Internet, make sure any new memory is compatible with the existing – if in doubt remove the old module and take it to a local computer shop. At the time of writing an extra 1GB of memory costs around £20–£30.

The memory module should be carefully pushed, without excessive force, into the slot in the motherboard, lining up the notch in the bottom edge of the module with the motherboard slot. You should hear the sound of the module clicking into the clips on the motherboard socket. If a memory module is not correctly located in its slot, the computer will "beep" when starting up.

Adding Extra USB 2.0 Ports

The USB ports are small rectangular sockets on the back and front of computers, as shown on the right. The  USB ports are used for connecting all sorts of devices such as printers, USB flash drives, digital cameras, etc. USB devices are very simple to connect and enable peripherals to be "hot-swapped", so you don't need to switch the computer off to plug in, for example, a digital camera. At the time of writing, USB 2.0, introduced in 2000, is the current standard, while USB 3.0 is just around the corner.

Many modern devices require USB 2.0 ports, while some computers are still using the earlier and slower USB 1.0 ports. However, it's easy to add some USB 2.0 ports to an older computer; these will allow you to connect lots of USB devices simultaneously. For example, I often connect a USB printer, two USB flash drives, a wireless keyboard dongle and mouse and a wireless network dongle.

You can fit a USB 2.0 PCI expansion card for £20 or less. It's just a case of removing the computer casing and carefully pushing the card into one of the spare PCI slots.

Setting Up a Wireless Network

The Network Router

A common way to connect a single computer to a broadband-enabled telephone line is via a device called an *ADSL modem*. ADSL is short for, in not very plain English, Asymmetric Digital Subscriber Line. However, many people are now replacing the ADSL modem with a *wireless router* as shown below.

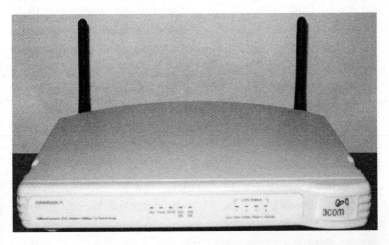

The router has its own power supply and connects to the broadband telephone line via a *microfilter*, shown on the right. Another socket in the microfilter allows an ordinary telephone handset to be connected to the microfilter. The handset can be used for

normal telephone calls while the computer is being used to browse the Internet.

Wireless routers have a built-in ADSL modem to provide the connection to the Internet; in addition several other computers can connect to the router wirelessly to share the single Internet connection. This is particularly useful if you have two or more computers and want to use them around your house or possibly work on a laptop in your garden.

Apart from the freedom that wireless networking gives, it's also easier to set up a wireless network since there are no cables to trail around your home and no holes to drill in walls. Even if you've only got one computer, it's still worth having a wireless router if you want to be able to use your computer in different rooms away from the telephone or cable socket.

The wireless router also has some Ethernet sockets which allow some computers to be linked by the older, more traditional Ethernet cables. These might be used to link some computers which are not likely to be moved.

For demanding work in business, the traditional "wired" Ethernet network has the greatest potential speed; also the wireless network can be vulnerable to hackers close to your home. People nearby, perhaps outside in the street with a laptop, can detect your wireless network and connect to your computer and the Internet unless you have secured it with a password or *security key*.

However, for general home use for browsing the Internet, sending e-mails, downloading sound and music, etc., a secure wireless network will perform more than adequately and will be much easier to install than the wired network.

Wireless routers can be bought for under £50 and are sometimes provided free when signing up with an Internet Service Provider such as BT or AOL.

Wireless Network Adaptors
Each computer on the network is connected to the router using a *wireless network adaptor*. The network adaptor can take the form of an expansion card as shown below.

Alternatively a wireless network adaptor may take the form of a *dongle*, as shown below. This plugs into a USB port on the back of the computer. A desktop stand and extension cable may be used to allow the wireless dongle to be moved to a position to give optimum signal strength.

The router package usually includes some Ethernet cables and these are also readily available from computer shops. A wireless router allows you to create a home network using a mixture of wireless and Ethernet connections.

During the initial setting up process, a computer is connected to the router by a cable and used to run the setup CD. The computer is connected to the router using either:

- A special USB cable from the router to a USB port on the computer.
- An Ethernet cable from the router to an Ethernet socket on the computer.

The Ethernet cable is generally regarded as the best way of connecting the router to a computer for the initial set-up process. Ethernet cables can be obtained or made up in various lengths; an 8 metre Ethernet cable is shown below.

Once the router is set up, any computer fitted with a wireless network adaptor can connect to the Internet from anywhere in the home.

Wi-Fi Range

Ranges of 50–300 metres from the router are often quoted by manufacturers but the range and signal strength are affected by obstructions such as walls and steel girders; however, you should be able to get a good Wi-Fi signal around most of an average sized house, flat and garden.

On our home network we have one machine next to the router connected by an Ethernet cable; three other machines plus a laptop can be used anywhere in the house or garden through wireless connections. Most laptops are "wireless ready" and can detect any nearby wireless network – they can also log on if the network is not secure.

Although the performance of wireless networking is not quite as fast as networking using Ethernet cables, we have found it perfectly satisfactory for surfing the Internet, e-mail and downloading large files. You can also print from any computer to a single printer serving the whole network.

Secure Wi-Fi Networks

If a neighbour has a wireless router, you may detect their network on your computer. Similarly, Internet "savvy" students and even criminals outside of your home could go online using your Internet connection and also look at files of personal and financial information.

The BT Home Hub wireless router uses a string of 10 letters and digits as a *wireless key*. The BT wireless key is printed on a label on the back of the Home Hub router.

The first time you use a computer to connect to the router you must enter the wireless key. The computer "remembers" the key for subsequent connections. Anyone using a different computer can't connect to the Internet via your router unless they enter the wireless key.

In the example below, my computer is connected to our BT Home Hub.

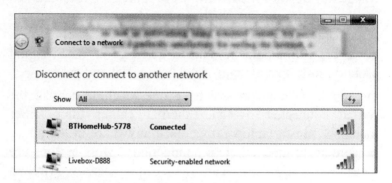

As shown above, my computer has also detected a neighbour's **Livebox** wireless network. If I click the **Livebox** network listed above, I will be unable to connect without entering the **Livebox security key** or **passphrase**.

Security keys such as these should prevent hackers from connecting to your wireless Internet connection.

Wi-Fi Hotspots

There are thousands of Wi-Fi *hotspots* or Internet *access points* in hotels, holiday cottages, stations, airports, etc. Modern laptops have a built-in wireless adaptor. To connect to the Internet, simply take the laptop within range of the hotspot and enter your username and password. With BT Total Broadband, you get several thousand minutes of free connection time per year on the BT Openzone network, with 10,000 hotspots in the UK and Ireland.

www.btopenzone.com

Tidying Up Your Desk

Save Space with a Flat Screen Monitor

If you've still got one of the old CRT (Cathode Ray Tube) monitors, it's a good idea to upgrade to one of the latest TFT (Thin Film Transistor) designs. Apart from freeing up acres of desk space, you are less likely to injure yourself moving it. The last two 19 inch CRT monitors I had were enormous and extremely difficult to move about. TFT monitors also use less power than their CRT ancestors.

A 19 inch TFT colour monitor can be bought for £90–£100; if you need a bigger screen and can afford it, the 20 inch and 22 inch models cost nearer £200. The size is measured diagonally across the screen. Picture quality is excellent and it's simply a case of plugging in the cables and letting Windows do the rest. Some flat screen monitors have built-in speakers – further reducing the amount of clutter on your desk caused by separate speakers and their cables.

Wireless Keyboards and Mice

I first acquired a wireless keyboard and mouse a few years ago and at that time was very disappointed. The main problem was that the batteries didn't seem to last very long at all and I soon reverted to the old cabled designs. However, several months ago I bought two Advent wireless mouse/keyboard sets at a cost of about £30 per set and they have proved excellent – I'm still using the original batteries.

The wireless mouse is a big improvement since it can be moved much more freely than the traditional cable design, which I find is restricted by the drag of the cable, especially when the desk is cluttered. The wireless keyboard also reduces the number of cables draped around the desk and can be used several feet away from the computer, perhaps on your lap. This might be an advantage if you're disabled or if desk space is limited. The mouse and keyboard are each powered by two ordinary AAA batteries and there's a warning light on the keyboard to indicate a low battery.

The wireless keyboard and mouse communicate with the computer via a wireless dongle receiver which plugs into an available USB port on the computer. Setting up time is minimal; it's just a case of installing the dongle and waiting for Windows to install the drivers. In the Advent kit, a CD containing the drivers is provided. Then the batteries should be installed in the mouse and keyboard, which should now be ready to use.

Index